the

BILDERBERG
CONSPIRACY

the

BILDERBERG CONSPIRACY

Inside the World's Most Powerful Secret Society

H. PAUL JEFFERS

CITADEL PRESS
Kensington Publishing Corp.
www.kensIngtonbooks.com

CITADEL PRESS BOOKS are published by

Kensington Publishing Corp.
119 West 40th Street
New York, NY 10018

All Kensington titles, imprints, and distributed lines are available at special quantity discounts for bulk purchases for sales promotions, premiums, fund-raising, educational, or institutional use. Special book excerpts or customized printings can also be created to fit specific needs. For details, write or phone the office of the Kensington special sales manager: Kensington Publishing Corp., 119 West 40th Street, New York, NY 10018, attn: Special Sales Department; phone 1-800-221-2647.

CITADEL PRESS and the Citadel logo are Reg. U.S. Pat. & TM Off.

First printing: August 2009

10 9 8 7 6 5 4 3 2 1

Printed in the United States of America

Library of Congress Control Number: 2009923868

ISBN-13: 978-0-8065-3115-1
ISBN-10: 0-8065-3115-0

CONTENTS

• Introduction •

"Man, This Is Just Evil"

Summoned to an urgent meeting in the U.S. Capitol on September 18, 2008, the Democrat and Republican leadership of both houses of Congress were informed by the secretary of the treasury, Henry "Hank" Paulson, and the chairman of the Federal Reserve Board, Ben Bernanke, of a "crisis" in the liquidity of the American banking system. They warned that the situation threatened the collapse of not only the nation's economy but the entire global financial structure. To avert such a calamity, Paulson proposed that the Congress authorize him, as treasury secretary, to acquire the bad debts on the books of banks and Wall Street firms in the amount of $700 billion. Before coming to Treasury, Paulson was chairman and chief executive officer of Goldman Sachs since the firm's initial public offering in 1999. He joined the Goldman Sachs Chicago office in 1974 and rose through the ranks, holding several positions including managing partner of the firm's Chicago office, co-head of the firm's investment banking division, president and chief operating officer, and co-senior partner.

Bernanke had served as chairman of the Federal Open Market Committee, the Federal Reserve system's principal monetary policymaking body. Before his appointment as chairman, he was chairman of the president's Council of Economic Advisers.

What Paulson and Bernanke had in common, aside from their positions as the federal overseers of the U.S. economy, was their affiliation with a secretive organization of international bankers, financiers, and top executives of global corporations known as the Bilderberg Group. Both had attended its most recent meeting in the Washington, DC, suburb of Chantilly, Virginia.

The objective of the Bilderbergers, according to its critics and a handful of journalists, is the elimination of national sovereignty, creation of a world government with a global currency, and consolidation of economic power by a small number of bankers. To achieve this "New World Order" and the goal of establishing global socialism, it was necessary to undermine the position of the United States as the only "superpower" of capitalism.

Typical of Bilderberg meetings was the gathering of the group in Canada in 2006. As the leading four-star hotel in Ottawa, Canada, the Brookstreet Hotel boasted that it "distinguishes itself through rapt attention to the smallest details, through impeccable service." It noted in its brochure that its 276 rooms, including 35 suites, were individually climate controlled and appointed with "stunning and sophisticated original works by past and present students of Ottawa's Canterbury Arts High School." The Au Naturel Spa provided "the perfect place to relax and unwind." A guest might "indulge" at the Perspectives Restaurant or lounge at the Options Bar listening to live music on weekends. The energetic could try out cycling and jogging paths; cross-country ski trails; the Marshes Golf Course—a Robert Trent Jones II design, rated as one of Canada's finest golf destinations—and the March Wood, a European PGA-approved short course. For those who preferred to play indoors, the hotel's recreational facilities included the Flex Fitness Studio with indoor and outdoor whirlpools and steam rooms. In every way, the hotel provided the sort of luxurious pampering to attract the rich, famous, and important personalities of show business, industry and government.

Consequently, it was not unusual on June 9, 2006, that such guests arrived in long, sleek limousines or bulky vans and sport utility vehicles with darkly tinted windows to ensure privacy. The hotel's serene suburban setting was suddenly transformed into what one observer called "a four-day festival of black suits, black limousines, burly security guards, and suspicions of world domination."

Alexander Panetta, a reporter for the *Canadian Press* of Ottawa, had been drawn to the Brookstreet Hotel by an unsigned press release, sent by fax, stating that a meeting of the Bilderberg Group would deal with energy issues, Iran, the Middle East, terrorism, immigration, Russia, European-American relations, and Asia. The announcement also provided a list of those attending that included financier and head of the Chase Bank David Rockefeller, former U.S. secretary of state Henry Kissinger, Queen Beatrix of Holland, New York governor George Pataki, the heads of Coca-Cola, Credit Suisse, Royal Bank of Canada, media moguls, world financiers, and cabinet ministers from Spain and Greece.

"The meeting is private to encourage frank and open discussion," said the release. "There will be no press conference."

Panetta wrote, "On the outskirts of the nation's capital, a tony high-rise hotel beside a golf course is hosting the annual meeting for one of the world's most secretive and powerful societies. It's not the Freemasons. Forget those fabled U.S. military men who tucked away UFOs in the Arizona desert. These guys, you've probably never even heard of, and if you believe the camera-toting followers who attend all their meetings, they control the world. They're called the Bilderberg Group. They include European royalty, national leaders, political power brokers and heads of the world's biggest companies." Ottawa police officers stood guard outside a dozen metal gates that served as security checkpoints a half a kilometer from the hotel. But the official force was clearly not in charge. To approach the hotel property, even uniformed officers had to show their credentials to the half-dozen black-suited men working for Globe Risk, a private security firm. "This is pretty unusual," said one Ottawa cop.

Another said they were hired to be there in their off-duty hours and weren't told much by their superiors: "They just told us these are important people and it's a private meeting." Panetta reported that a small crowd of curious onlookers snapped photos of black-windowed sedans stopping at the checkpoints. It was impossible to see who was sitting inside, but fun to imagine. Nor was the Bilderberg logo anywhere to be seen, except for nondescript white placards stamped with the letter *B* and tucked under all those tinted windshields.

Even the hotel barred members of the hotel gym from the premises. A sign was placed on the gym door informing them the facilities would be closed for four days. All the other hotel guests were asked to check out. Any vehicles remaining in the parking lot would be towed.

Conspicuous among the small group of curious onlookers as the limousines and vans arrived was seventy-four-year-old American journalist James P. Tucker. Editor of the *American Free Press*, he had been following the Bilderberg group for decades and written extensively about it, including his recently published *Jim Tucker's Bilderberg Diary*. Standing outside the hotel, he described to other journalists details of what he had learned of the group's inner workings.

"Some people say that I advocate a conspiracy theory," he said. "That's not true. I recognize a conspiracy fact."

Another Bilderberg watcher, Daniel Estulin, snapped photographs of every vehicle that approached the Brookstreet Hotel. Author of *The True Story of the Bilderberg Group*, he had been investigating the Bilderberg Group for fifteen years. Living in Spain because he said he was fearful of reprisals for his criticisms, he ventured to the sites of the Group's annual meetings and claimed to have sources who provided the details of the gatherings and names of attendees.

Alex Jones, a documentary filmmaker from Texas, directed his crew to turn their camera on a passing limo with a *B* in its windshield and muttered, "Man, this is evil." Two years earlier, the Bilderberg Group had marked its fiftieth anniversary. "For four days some of the West's chief political movers, business leaders, bankers, industrialists, and strategic thinkers got together at a five-star hotel in northern Italy." One of the speakers was reported to be Senator John Edwards. He was so well received, said Bilderberg critics, that the Group saw to it that Edwards became John Kerry's vice-presidential running mate in 2004. The Group has also been credited with the elections of Jimmy Carter, Bill Clinton, and both George H. W. Bush and his son to the presidency. The Group is also said to have been the motivating force behind the rise of Margaret Thatcher and Tony Blair to be British prime minister.

Some of the suspicion surrounding the Bilderberg Group stems from the fact that one of founders was a Rockefeller and an early and continuing member is Henry Kissinger. One critic noted, "One can't help but wonder, when Bilderberg organizers, including David Rockefeller, Henry Kissinger and the rest, have completed their project of enclosing all global goods and services into their own hands what else they are up to."

The suspicion of outsiders is that the Bilderbergers are conniving to control the world. In that they are not the first secretive group believed to consist of a society's elite whose purpose was to run everything and to control the destiny of the world. Secret societies have been around as long as civilization. It's from a biblical-times elite known as Cabalists that we have the word "cabal," defined in the Merriam-Webster's dictionary as "the artifices and intrigues of a group of persons secretly united in a plot (as to overturn a government); *also*: a group engaged in such artifices and intrigues."

In Greek and Roman times, equivalents of the Bilderberg Group were mystery cults, usually with religious overtones. During the Middle Ages, stonemasons who built cathedrals and other public buildings formed into "lodges" that were the cornerstones of the later and modern Freemasonry. The Crusades gave rise to Knights Templar, so-called because of their headquarters at the ruins of Solomon's Temple in Jerusalem. Said to be possessors of a secret that enabled the Order to became so fabulously rich that they invented international banking and were able to dictate to kings and popes, they remain history's most mysterious and romanticized secret society.

The nineteenth century brought the Illuminati. Meaning enlightened, it was founded in Germany soon after 1776 by Adam Weishaupt and had close affinities with the Freemasons. It was briefly very popular among German rationalists. Dissolved in 1785 by the government of Bavaria, Weishaupt's Illuminati is said to have been an influence on Thomas Jefferson and other Founding Fathers. Although the Illuminati today are described as elite men who control the international bankers and work behind the scenes at all levels of business, politics, government, and journalism to control the world, the actual Illuminati Order (IO) of today claims that it "has evolved into a global network that promotes a general knowledge and acceptance of the concept of individual rights and the proper role of government as protector of these rights." Its website also states, "We work together to spread the seeds of freedom far and wide."

Other present-day secret societies that arouse suspicions that conspiracy is afoot are the Roman Catholic Opus Dei and the mysterious secular group at Yale University with the ominous name "Skull & Bones."

Virtually unknown outside Roman Catholicism until the book and movie *The DaVinci Code*, and formally known as The Prelature of the Holy Cross, Opus Dei is an organization that teaches the Catholic belief that everyone is called to holiness and that ordinary life is a path to sanctity. A majority of its membership are lay people, with priests under the governance of a prelate appointed by the Pope. Opus Dei is Latin for *Work of God*. Founded in Spain in 1928 by a priest, Josemaría Escrivá, it was given final approval in 1950 by Pope Pius XII. In 1982, the Church made it into a personal prelature. It has approximately 87,000 members in more than eighty countries. About 70 percent of the members live in their private homes and live regular lives, while the remainder of the members are celibate and primarily live in the Opus Dei centers. "Its mission," asserts its website, "is to help people turn their work and daily activities into occasions for growing closer to God, for serving others, and for improving society. Opus Dei complements the work of local churches by offering classes, talks, retreats and pastoral care that help people develop their personal spiritual life and apostolate."

High on the list of organizations suspected of being involved in the construction of a global network of the elite to run the world, Skull & Bones is believed to be an incubator for the American "establishment." Alexandra Robbins, author of *Secrets of the Tomb: Skull and Bones, the Ivy League, and the Hidden Paths of Power*, said that it is "America's most powerful secret society." Based at Yale, where it is headquartered in a building called the Tomb, it has included among its members, presidents, including George W. Bush, and George H. W. Bush, as well as William Howard Taft, Supreme Court Chief Justices of the United States, CIA officials, cabinet members, congressmen and senators, as well as George W. Bush's 2004 opponent, Senator John Kerry. There are only 800 living members. "One of the interesting and I think disturbing things about Skull and Bones." said Robbins, "is that its purpose is to get members into positions of power and have those members hire other members into prestigious positions."

In May 2007, CIA historians publicly released an article that rebutted inaccurate but enduring beliefs that Skull & Bones was an incubator of the U.S. Intelligence Community. The CIA article noted that movies such as *The Good Shepherd* perpetuated in the public mind the notion that entry into CIA's upper echelons hinged on membership in Skull & Bones. While the society may not have been the cradle for future CIA operatives or the World War II Office of Strategic Services (OSS, predecessor to the CIA), it is accurate to note that a disproportionate number of Yale graduates led and staffed the intelligence community, including George H. W. Bush, director of Central Intelligence (January 30, 1976–January 20, 1977). It is said that the term "spook" once designated a Yale senior or secret society member.

While there is no discernable correlation between Skull & Bones, the CIA and the Bilderberg Group, the Conservative Movement pioneer and founder/editor of the *National Review*, William F. Buckley, Jr., was a member of all three. It is also a matter of record that the CIA in the first year of the Eisenhower administration had a significant role in fostering United States participation in the founding of the Bilderberg Group.

Since the start of the Bilderberg Group in Europe in 1954, suspicions have grown that it brought together "the political leadership of the Western world," heads of global corporations, international bankers and financiers, prominent journalists, media moguls and those who shape public opinion in order to establish "a New World Order." The goal was said to be the "abolition of national sovereignty, creation of a global monetary system, and the establishment of a world government that they devise, control, and profit from."

Journalists who have sought to learn the truth about the Bilderberg Group have run into a wall of silence. Assigned to report on the fiftieth anniversary of its founding, Jonathan Duffy of the British Broadcasting Corporation (BBC) wrote in its *Online Magazine* in 2004 that because of the Group's secrecy "an extraordinary conspiracy theory has grown up around the Group that alleges the fate of the world is largely decided by Bilderberg." In Yugoslavia, leading Serbs have blamed Bilderberg for triggering the war that led to the downfall of Slobodan Milosevic. Oklahoma City bomber Timothy McVeigh and Osama Bin Laden were reported to have bought into the theory that Bilderberg pulls the strings with which national governments dance. While hard-line right-wingers and libertarians accuse Bilderberg of being a liberal Zionist plot, leftists such as activist Tony Gosling are equally critical. A former journalist, Mr. Gosling runs a campaign against the group from his home in Bristol, England. "My main problem is the secrecy," he explained. "When so many people with so much power get together in one place I think we are owed an explanation of what is going on."

Bilderberg insiders scoff at the conspiracy believers. Privacy, rather than secrecy is key to such a meeting explained *Financial Times* journalist Martin Wolf. Invited to Bilderberg meetings several times in a nonreporting role, he asserted, "It's not an executive body. No decisions are taken there."

As an up-and-coming statesman in the 1950s, Denis Healey, who went on to become a British Labour Party government official, was one of the four founding members of Bilderberg. His response to claims that the group exerts a shadowy hand on the global tiller is met with characteristic bluntness. "Crap! There's absolutely nothing in it," Healey exclaimed. "We never sought to reach a consensus on the big issues at Bilderberg. It's simply a place for discussion."

Healey asserted that the Bilderberg Group was formed in the spirit of Post–World War II trans-Atlantic cooperation, and that the idea behind Bilderberg was that future wars could be prevented by bringing power brokers together in an informal setting away from prying eyes.

"Bilderberg is the most useful international group I ever attended," he said. "In my experience the most useful meetings are those when one is free to speak openly and honestly."

Those who defend Bilderberg Group secrecy point out that when America's Founding Fathers met in Philadelphia's Independence Hall to draft the Constitution of the United States, they did so behind locked doors.

Although suspected conspiracies can be dated to ancient Rome and Greece and the later Illuminati and Freemasonry, there has never been a secret organization with the global reach of the Bilderberg Group and its membership consisting of individuals with so much personal, corporate, governmental, and mass media power. Those who express suspicions of the Group also note that it appears to have an intimate association with organizations such as the American Council on Foreign Relations and the Trilateral Commission that promote the goal of globalization and a New World Order at the expense of national sovereignty and individual liberty under a world government.

A press release (see p. 217) announcing the 2006 Bilderberg Group meeting in Ottawa described the organization as a benign annual forum for a "broad cross section of leading citizens. . . . assembled for nearly three days of informal and off-the-record discussion about topics of current concern especially in the fields of foreign affairs and the international economy." The privacy (secrecy) of the meetings, said the press release, was intended solely for the purpose of allowing all the "participants to speak their minds openly and freely." In furtherance of this policy, the Group issued no statement at the end of the conference and held no press conference. As limousines and other vehicles departed with windows darkened to shield the occupants from the gaze of curious onlookers, and the Brookstreet Hotel was again open to the public, the perception that remained was that the Bilderberg Group was a sinister conspiracy of the world's power elite.

The purpose of this book is to explore objectively what is known about the Bilderberg Group, examine its history and stated goals, weigh allegations that it is a dangerous conspiracy, evaluate the nature and possible motives of its critics, look at the Group's membership, and assess its influence, if any, since its inception.

A tale as murky as any good spy novel, the story of the Bilderberg Group began with the emergence onto the world stage of a mysterious figure out of the shadowy history of eastern Europe when the world was frozen in the grip of the Cold War.

· One ·

THE PATRIOT AND THE PRINCE

In a comic drama titled *The History Boys* by British playwright Alan Bennett that became a hit in London's West End and on Broadway and was made into a movie, eight students prepare for admission examinations for Oxford University. One of the youths whose interests lie more in sports than in academics is asked to give his definition of history. After a moment of deep and anguished contemplation, he replies, "How do I define history? It's just one fucking thing after another."

The definition applies to the extraordinary adventures of an exiled intellectual Polish patriot who is acknowledged as the father of the Bilderberg Group.

The series of events began two months before Joseph Hieronymus Retinger's birth on April 17, 1888, in Krakow in the province of the Austro-Hungarian Empire that was then known as Galicia, but on future maps of Europe would be called Poland.

In an address to the German parliament on February 6, 1888, Prince von Bismarck boasted, "We Germans fear God and nothing else in the world."

This bravado was based in large measure on a military pact between Germany, Italy, and Austria-Hungary. Known as the Triple Alliance, it pledged mutual assistance if any one of the three parties found itself at war with Russia, Great Britain, or France or a combination. Reigning over Germany as the prince addressed the Reichstag, the emperor who had signed the treaty, Kaiser Wilhelm I, was just six months short of his ninety-first birthday and had ruled twenty-seven years. When he died on March 9, 1888, the crown passed to his fifty-seven-year-old son Friedrich Wilhelm. Terminally ill with throat cancer and unable to speak, he died on June 15 and was succeeded by his twenty-nine-year-old son, Wilhelm II.

Twenty-four years after this series of deaths in the year of Joseph H. Retinger's birth, that in European history became known as "the year of the three emperors," Kaiser Wilhelm invoked the terms of the treaty to assist Austro-Hungary in a war with Russia. Because Russia had a mutual defense alliance with Great Britain and France, the result was World War I. The effect of the subjugation of his native land on Retinger was a desire to put an end to European conflicts through a unification of the continent that would ensure independence for Poland.

The youngest of four children of Józef Stanislaw Retinger, the private legal counsel and advisor to the eminent Polish nobleman Count Wladyslaw Zamoyski, he was a bright youth with an interest in studies that seemed to point him toward the priesthood. When his father died, he was taken under Count Zamoyski's wing and enrolled in a seminary, but soon concluded that he could never keep a vow of celibacy.

With the count's financial support, he went to Paris in 1906 to study at the Sorbonne.

As a handsome eighteen-year-old student in the École des Sciences Politiques, with an impeccable connection to nobility, he found himself warmly welcomed into Parisian society. His new friends included the Marquis de Castellane and a circle of bright young artists, painters, musicians, and writers. When he wasn't spending his afternoons and evenings in the plush salons of the French aristocracy or sipping wine in Left Bank cafes, he found himself hearing new compositions by Maurice Ravel and François Poulenc or reading the latest manu-scripts of François Mauriac and André Gide. Proving to his benefactor that none of these delightful diversions interfered with his studies, he proudly reported to Count Zamoyski in 1908 that he had earned his Docteur des Lettres in Political Science, giving him the distinction at twenty years old of being the youngest recipient of a Ph.D. in the history of the Sorbonne. Continuing his education at the University of Munich, he studied comparative psychology. Returning to Krakow in 1912, he started a literary monthly and married a beautiful Polish girl, Otylia Zubrzycka.

With the likelihood of war, he was asked by a group of activists for Polish independence, called the Supreme National Council, to open a bureau in London to advocate the Polish cause. Patriots, idealists, and dreamers, they envisioned an outcome of the war that would bring the dismantling of the Austro-Hungarian Empire. This would mean a re-drawing of the map of Europe in which the empire's former provinces would take their places in the new world as independent countries. But for Retinger, the dream of an independent Poland included a hope that the new nations of postwar Europe would fashion a system in which they would never again wage war with one another.

As he had done in Paris, Retinger developed not only political friendships, but a circle of artistic and literary companions. His closest association was with the renowned Polish writer Joseph Conrad, author of *The Heart of Darkness* and *Lord Jim*. While Retinger and Conrad and their wives were vacationing in Galicia in the summer of 1914, Austria-Hungary and Russia and Russia's ally, Germany, went to war. Bound by the Triple Alliance, Great Britain and France declared war on Germany and Russia, and World War I was underway. For Retinger, the conflict was welcomed as an opportunity to use his political contacts in England and France to persuade Austria to split from the empire and make peace, opening the door for Poland to gain its independence.

Declared persona non grata by Austria, branded an enemy with a death penalty imposed by Germany, and unwelcome in England, penniless, he fled to Spain and then to Mexico.

Now in his thirties, Retinger followed the pattern he developed in Paris and London of associating with artists, writers, intellectuals and the politically motivated. Among the friends he made were Luis Napoléon Morones, leader of the Regional Conference of Mexican Workers (CROM), and Plutarco Elias Calles, who later became President of Mexico. Because of this friendship, Retinger was asked by the Mexican government to mediate a dispute between the United States and Mexico over American oil company rights. In these travels on behalf of Mexico to the United States, he developed friendships with American leaders, including future associate justice of the Supreme Court Justice Felix Frankfurter, who helped him obtain a new Polish passport.

Again free to travel in Europe, Retinger was in London on September 1, 1939, when Germany invaded Poland. With the formation of a Polish government in exile in London, he became the principal political advisor to the prime minister, General Wladyslaw Sikorski.

In the Fall of 1941, he accompanied Sikorski to North Africa to visit the embattled soldiers of the Polish Carpathian regiment as they held out with British and other forces against the siege by Germany's General Erwin Rommel's Afrika Korps of the Tunisian seaport of Tobruk.

Three years later, at the age of fifty-six, he parachuted into his occupied homeland. In Operation Salamander, he was the oldest person to ever parachute on a wartime mission. He wore a British uniform and carried identity papers in the name of Captain Paisley. According to one account of the mission, members of the Polish-exile Home Army were suspicious of Retinger and ordered him liquidated during the mission. They arranged for two key containers of equipment to disappear. The plane took off streaming fuel. Retinger was robbed of his papers and prevented from boarding another crucial plane. A nurse/assassin named Izabela Horodecka was to give him a lethal substance, but gave him only half the dose. Retinger survived the poisoning, but was delayed by two months in returning to London. Paralyzed for several months, he convalesced at the Dorchester Hotel.

When not out of London on missions, Retinger organized exiled ministers of foreign affairs who settled in Britain and began promoting a postwar European Union (EU). Many of these discussions were over lunch in the Claridges Hotel, with Dutch prince Bernhard presiding. An outcome of talks held at the Savoy Hotel in 1944 was the formation of the Benelux Union (Netherlands, Belgium and Luxembourg).

With war over, Retinger was present for a conference at Chatham House, the subject being "A European Continent." In early May 1946, he left for Brussels to join with Belgian minister Paul van Zeeland at a meeting of the European League of Economical Co-operation, to which American representatives were invited. In 1947, he began making preparations for a Congress of Europe at The Hague in May 1948. Among attendees were Winston Churchill, Konrad Adenauer of West Germany, British prime minster Anthony Eden, and philosopher Bertrand Russell. From May 7–11, 1948, delegates from around Europe and observers from Canada and the United States gathered in the Netherlands for meetings presided over by Churchill that brought together eight hundred representatives from across a broad political spectrum, providing them with the opportunity to discuss ideas about development of the EU. A call was made for a political, economic, and monetary Union of Europe. This conference was to have a profound influence on the shape of the European Movement, which was formally created on October 25, 1948. Described by one participant as "the personal work of Retinger," the Congress laid the foundation for the formation, nine months later, of the Council of Europe that laid the groundwork for a European parliament.

With a doctorate from the Sorbonne in political science, Dr. Joseph Retinger knew that the idea of European unity was nothing new.

"The philosopher Montesquieu said in the 18th century, 'Whenever in the past Europe has been united by force, the unity lasted no longer than the space of a single reign.'....

"In 1871, the French novelist Victor Hugo implored, 'Let us have the United States of Europe; let us have continental federation; let us have European freedom.'"

"In 1922, Count Richard Coudenhove-Kalergi founded the Pan European Union.

"In 1941, Andre Malraux had called for a 'European New Deal' that envisioned a federal Europe without the U.S.S.R.

"In an October 1942 letter to the British War Cabinet, Churchill wrote. 'Hard as it is to say now, I trust that the European family may act unitedly as one under a Council of Europe. I look forward to a United States of Europe.'

"In a September 19, 1946 speech at the University of Zurich he asserted, 'We must build a kind of United States of Europe.' "

In large measure because of Retinger, at the Congress of Europe at The Hague in The Netherlands nearly a thousand prominent Europeans from sixteen countries had called for establishment of a United Europe. In July 1948, he went to the United States with Churchill, diplomat Duncan Sandys, and former Belgian prime minister Paul-Henri Spaak to raise money for the movement. This led to the establishment of the American Committee on a United Europe on March 29, 1949. Their first Chairman was William Donovan, the first director of the wartime OSS. The vice chairman was Allen Dulles, who was to become the director of the CIA.

Retinger noted that in a "historic address on June 5, 1947, General George C. Marshall, U.S. secretary of state, made proposals for European aid know as "the Marshall Plan," that also called for the unification of Europe."

"On March 17, 1948, a fifty-year treaty signed in Brussels by England, France, Belgium, The Netherlands, and Luxembourg, called for 'collaboration in economic, social, and cultural matters and for collective self defense.'

"On May 5, 1949, Foreign Ministers from ten European countries signed a treaty in London, for the purpose of working for 'greater European unity, to improve the conditions of life and principle human values in Europe and to uphold the principles of parliamentary democracy, the rule of law and human rights.' The Treaty sought to promote unity, both socially and economically." Its members were Belgium (1949), Denmark (1949), France (1949), Ireland (1949), Italy (1949), Luxembourg (1949), Netherlands (1949), Norway (1949), Sweden (1949), England (1949), Greece (1949), Turkey (1949), Iceland (1949), and West Germany (1951). "The Council of Europe was open to all European States which accepted the 'principles of the rule of law and of the enjoyment by all persons within (their) jurisdiction of human rights and fundamental freedoms.' "With headquarters in Strasbourg, France, ministers met twice a year, their deputies met ten times a year, and 154 delegates met at the Congresses.

In 1949, "the North Atlantic Treaty Organization (NATO)... was a defense alliance meant to implement the North Atlantic Treaty and to apply counterpressure against the growing Soviet presence.

"On May 27, 1952, the European Defense Community Treaty was signed in Paris, and provided for the armies of West Germany, France, Italy, Belgium, the Netherlands, and Luxembourg, to become closely aligned with England's."

In the years since Retinger began promoting the cause of European unity in wartime London, hopes that the Soviet Union would be a partner in peace had been dashed. In late 1952, the Red Army remained where it had stood in 1945. The Iron Curtain that Churchill described in a 1946 speech as stretching from the Baltic to the Adriatic remained in place. "Behind it," said Churchill, "lie all the capitals of the ancient states of Central and Eastern Europe. Warsaw, Berlin, Prague, Vienna, Budapest, Belgrade, Bucharest and Sofia."

Described by friends and himself as an eminence grise (gray eminence) as he moved through the corridors of power in Europe and worked on behalf of unifying countries that had warred with one another for centuries, the Polish patriot faced the brutal reality that Poland and all the nations of Eastern Europe were now Soviet captives, and that in a confrontation with the Soviet Union known as the Cold War, the freedom of Europe, united or not, depended on the United States of America.

The Cold War was at its chilliest. As unshakeable as the granite pillars of the Kremlin, Josef Stalin ruled the Soviet Union and its Eastern European satellites with all the power and ferocity of the czars of Russia. In the face of the threat of a Soviet attack, pressure for German rearmament was mounting and creating tensions and stresses in Europe.

Because Retinger always believed that public opinion followed the lead of influential individuals, he decided in the early part of 1952 to consult friends who shared his view that the future of Europe depended on unity of purpose between nations. In discussions with Paul van Zeeland and Paul Rykens, who was then chairman of Unilever, it was agreed on the need to find the right person to take a leading part in rallying influential leaders to the cause of European unity. The person Retinger had in mind was Prince Bernhard of the Netherlands. Because they had met briefly during the Congress of the Hague, Retinger knew that the Prince was interested in politics and supported European unity. Although his official position of Prince Consort to the Queen of the Netherlands limited his freedom of political action, he was always ready to help good causes. His support would be invaluable.

"The elder son of Prince Bernhard Casimir of Lippe Biesterfeld and Baroness Armgard von Sierstorpff-Cramm, a member of an old Bavarian family, Bernard was brought up on the family estate in Brandenburg, near the Polish frontier, sharing tutors with his younger brother and attending the gymnasium at Züllichau. After completing his schooling at the Arndt classical gymnasium in Berlin, he spent some time at Lausanne University perfecting his French (English had been his first language) and then studied international commercial law at Munich and Berlin universities." With the rise of Nazism in Germany, "Bernhard compromised with the demands of Hitlerism by joining the Motorized SS in Berlin."

Graduating "in 1935, the year after his father's death, he resigned from the SS and entered the service of I G Farben, the German chemical combine, in its Paris office." It was "while he was there that the Dutch Minister in Lisbon suggested that he call on Queen Wilhelmina and her daughter, Princess Juliana, when they were all in Garmisch-Partenkirchen for the Olympic Winter Games of 1935. It was later recorded on the Prince's authority that he found the Princess 'terribly sweet, very shy, extremely intelligent and very much dominated by her mother.' The announcement of their engagement on September 8, 1936, after about a year's friendship, came as a surprise to the Dutch public. Bernhard was 25 and Juliana 27.

"The Netherlands, neutral in the First World War, was at this time maintaining a stoutly impartial attitude to events in Germany. When Bernhard made his protocol call before giving up German nationality, however, Hitler received him coldly, and thereafter the Nazis picked on insignificant Dutch demonstrations of interest in the Princess's fiancé as affronts to Germany. There was even a threat to withhold the passports of German guests to the wedding. Bernhard's energetic personal intervention on this occasion won him Dutch esteem.

"The wedding took place in The Hague on January 7, 1937, and Bernhard took his place in the House of Orange, one of the richest dynasties in the world. During the engagement Queen Wilhelmina had agreed that Bernhard should be spared the fate of her own husband, Prince Heinrich of Mecklenburg-Schwerin, whose participation in public affairs had been limited to chairmanship of the Dutch Red Cross.

"Bernhard's first duties were military, but his training was delayed by a bad motor accident at the end of November 1937. However, immediately after the outbreak of war in September 1939, Queen Wilhelmina appointed him, though still only with the rank of captain, to inspect and report to her personally on the state of the defenses of the still neutral Netherlands.

"Two days after Germany invaded the Netherlands on May 10, 1940, Queen Wilhelmina ordered Bernhard to take his wife and their two daughters, Beatrix and Irene, to England." Within a week, and against the wishes of the Queen, who had followed them almost immediately into exile, Bernhard was back in the Netherlands, but he discovered there was no hope of creating a useful resistance. He was able to make his second escape to England in a British patrol boat.

During the war he "became chief liaison officer between the British and Dutch Armed Forces. He visited and encouraged Dutch military and naval units in training in Britain, Canada and the United States, and Dutch airmen serving with the RAF. . . . He became known to the British public for his War Weapons Fund, paid for by people in the Dutch overseas empire, which was used to buy bombers and fighters for the RAF and the Royal Netherlands Navy." He then won British hearts by becoming an RAF fighter pilot.

"In September 1944, when liberation seemed nearer than it was, Bernhard was appointed Supreme Commander of the Netherlands Armed Forces. This excluded the navy but included the Dutch Resistance Movement." His relations with the Supreme Allied Commander, General Dwight D. Eisenhower, were good, but he blamed British commander Bernard L. Montgomery, for the failure and heavy losses of a parachute attack called Operation Market Garden on the city of Arnhem in 1944.

When Queen Wilhelmina abdicated the throne, Juliana succeeded to the crown, but as Prince Consort, Bernhard continued as chairman of the Joint Chiefs of Staff, while increasingly turning his attention to stimulating Dutch industry and Dutch trade overseas. Visits abroad provided the background for an enterprise that interested him greatly, so a conference of statesmen, businessmen and intellectuals from Europe and America proposed by Retinger was of great interest. During their first meeting, the Prince was sympathetic and intrigued by the project. He wanted to think it over and consult his advisers and friends. Other meetings took place, more people were consulted, and soon a small select group of people became involved.

At a meeting in Paris on September 25, 1952, everyone agreed that there was an urgent need to do something to improve relations with the United States.

According to biographer Kai Bird in *The Chairman: John J. McCoy, The Making of the American Establishment,* in late 1952 "Retinger went to America to try the idea out on his American contacts. Among others, he saw such old friends as diplomat Averell Harriman, banker David Rockefeller, and General Walter Bedell Smith, then director of the CIA. After Retinger explained his proposal, Smith said, 'Why the hell didn't you come to me in the first place?' He quickly referred Retinger to C. D. Jackson, who was about to become [President] Eisenhower's special assistant for psychological warfare to the United States. It took a while for Jackson to organize the American wing of the group." Eisenhower, the new president, as well as some of his closest collaborators had a recent experience of Europe and appreciated its problems. They knew Bernhard well and held him in high esteem. As a result of this, an American group was quickly brought together under the chairmanship of the late John Coleman, president of the Burroughs Corporation, assisted by Joseph Johnson, director of the Carnegie Foundation. With America on board, the way was cleared for the most unique conference of world leaders ever contemplated.

All that had to be decided was its location.

Two

YOU ARE CORDIALLY INVITED

The Dutch village of Oosterbeek in the province of Gelderland is part of the municipality of Renkum and lying about five kilometers west of the northern bank of the River Rhine. "The oldest part of the village is the Benedendorp (Lower Village). Parts of the church known as the Hervormde Kerk (Reformed Church) date back to the second half of the tenth century. In the nineteenth, several mansions were built on the higher ground to the north of the old village." But for the men on the guest list for a conference to which Prince Bernhard was inviting them in May 1954, the region was best known for a military disaster in September 1944.

In the largest airborne drop in history, called Operation Market Garden, an attempt to capture a bridge across the Rhine at the city of Arnhem by American, British, Canadian and Polish troops had ended in a disastrous withdrawal, with a large amount of the fighting carried out in and around Oosterbeek. Looking as if nothing had happened, the Hotel de Bilderberg stood serenely amid ancient trees and offered exactly the tranquil setting for serious men to gather in pampered comfort to contemplate the state of a troubled and dangerous world and speculate on the ways and means to shape a brighter, more prosperous, peaceful, and orderly planet.

The list of guests drawn up by Prince Bernhard, Retinger, and others consisted of "eighty participants, including some twenty Americans." Behind closed doors and drawn drapes would assemble "prominent politicians, industrialists, bankers, writers, unionists and scholars. Prince Bernhard, Paul van Zeeland, and John Coleman would take the chair in turn. An atmosphere of tense expectation, to be expected when important men gathered together for the first time to warily feel their way was soon dissipated, thanks primarily to the charm, easy manner, and sense of humor of the royal host. Speakers were only allowed five minutes at a time, which helped to liven up debates, while 'the pungent interventions of C. D. Jackson of the United States, Denis Healey and Lord Boothby from Great Britain, and a few others added bite to the discussions.' "

Born in New York City on March 16, 1902, Charles Douglas Jackson graduated from Yale in 1924 and went into the marble and stone import business. In 1931, he became president of Time Incorporated. After holding several government posts in World War II, he became managing director of Time-Life International and, in 1949, publisher of *Fortune Magazine*. After two years as president of the Free Europe Committee and director of Radio Free Europe (1951–1952), he served as a speechwriter for Republican presidential candidate Dwight Eisenhower.

Upon Eisenhower's election, he was named to the Committee on International Information Activities. From "February 16, 1953 to March 31, 1954, he was Special Assistant to the President for International Affairs, with responsibility loosely defined as international affairs, Cold War planning, and psychological warfare. His main function was the coordination of activities aimed at interpreting world situations to the best advantage of the United States and her allies and exploiting incidents which reflected negatively on the Soviet Union, Communist China and other enemies in the Cold War." This position required close coordination with representatives of the State and Defense departments, the U.S. Information Agency, the president's Special Assistant for National Security Affairs, and the CIA.

Described as an idea man and one of the most colorful figures in the administration, he was said to have given Eisenhower "brash advice on how to deal with the Soviets."

The son of an engineer, Denis Healey was born in Keighley, Yorkshire, in 1917. When he was eight years old, he won a scholarship to Bradford Grammar School. Influenced by the poetry of Wilfred Owen and Siegfried Sassoon from World War I, he became a pacifist and in 1935 resigned from the school's Officer's Training Corps. In 1936, he entered Balliol College, Oxford. Active in politics, he rejected his pacifism and joined the Communist Party. He later wrote on *The Time of My Life*, "For the young in those days, politics was a world of simple choices. The enemy was Hitler with his concentration camps. The objective was to prevent a war by standing up to Hitler. Only the Communist Party seemed unambiguously against Hitler. The [Neville] Chamberlain Government was for appeasement. Labour seemed torn between pacifism and a half-hearted support for collective security, and the Liberals did not count."

"With the outbreak of the Second World War, Healey joined the British Army and served with the Royal Engineers in North Africa, Sicily and Italy. This included being Military Landing Officer to the British assault brigade at Anzio. By the end of the war he had reached the rank of major." Having "left the Communist Party during the war, he joined the Labour Party." In the 1945 general election, as a candidate for Parliament for the towns of "Pudsey and Otley, he lost by 1,651 votes. In November, 1945, he became secretary of the International Department of the Labour Party." In 1952, he was successful in being elected to the House of Commons.

Healey recalled, "Retinger was a small wizened man, with a pince-nez

on a wrinkled brown face. He was crippled by polio. . . . Convinced of
the need for a similar forum to strengthen unity between Europe and
North America, he approached Hugh Gaitskell, General Colin Gub-
bins, who had commanded SOE [Special Operation Europe] during
the war, and several leading politicians and businessmen who were concerned to strengthen Atlantic cooperation. They asked Prince Bernhard
of the Netherlands to act as Chairman, because they rightly thought it
would be difficult to find a politician whose objectivity would be above
suspicion, and who could call Cabinet ministers from any country to
order without causing offense."

Healey noted that "the Bilderberg conferences inevitably aroused
jealousy, because they were exclusive, and suspicion, because they were
private. In America they were attacked as a left-wing plot to subvert the
United States, in Europe as a capitalist plot to undermine socialism.
They were neither. Immense care was taken to invite a fair balance from
all political parties, and to include trade unionists as well as businessmen.

"Though the discussions were more carefully prepared than at many
such meetings," said Healey, "I myself wrote a paper for most conferences—their real value, as always, was in the personal contacts made
outside the conference hall. Industrialists like Giovanni Agnelli [Italy]
and Otto Wolff von Amerongen [Germany] had to listen to socialists
and trade unionists and vice versa. Experience has taught me that lack
of understanding is the main cause of all evil in public affairs—as in
private life. Nothing is more likely to produce understanding than the
sort of personal contact which involves people not just as officials or
representatives, but also as human beings."

In addition to the meetings, meals and drinks were occasions for
some of the most interesting, stimulating, and amusing exchanges. After three days of living together in this secluded place, which participants left only once, when Bernhard invited them to cocktails at the
Royal Palace nearby, a certain faint but discernible bond was created.

A new entity was born. But it was difficult to define what it was. Its purpose, its methods and its structure were new and original. They did not bear any analogy and did not fit into any known category.

For the time being, "it was called the Bilderberg Group after the name of the hotel in which the first meeting took place. The name has stuck and remained in use.

"Since the first conference in 1954, many others were held under the Chairmanship of Prince Bernhard, usually at yearly intervals, and each time in a different country, including the United States and Canada. The subjects discussed varied, but always covered the problems which confronted the Western countries and which are likely to create friction and divergences between them."

"It is perhaps the best forum possible to debate the great issues of the day," said Healey. "It is certainly one of the best informed assemblies, and after a Bilderberg weekend one leaves with a feeling of knowing not only the points of view within the different countries but, what is more important, having had an insight into the inner feelings of the principal actors."

"Yet the importance of the Bilderberg Group stemmed from the people who took part. At each successive meeting, new participants were invited. Only the inner circle, called the Steering Committee, which became responsible for the preparation of the meetings, remained the same and even there a change of guard occasionally took place. During the first three or four years the all-important selection of participants was a delicate and difficult task. This was particularly so as regards politicians. It was not easy to persuade top office holders to come. The occasion was interesting and pleasant enough but was it worth a four day foreign journey?"

Retinger displayed great skill and an uncanny ability to pick out people who in a few years time were to accede to the highest offices in their respective countries. "In this way after a few years, when the fame of the conferences began to spread, getting people to come was no longer a problem. The opposite was the case. Then the most frequent problem was how to keep them out without creating offense.

"After several years, the Bilderberg Group would claim an impressive array of statesmen and potentates of all sorts, who at one stage or another have been brought into its circle. The character, the strength and the vitality of any group depended on the growth of a network of personal relations between its members. In the early days Retinger was largely the focus and the intermediary in addition to being the moving spirit."

"Within a few years, however," observed Healey, "Prince Bernhard became the true center of all the loyalties and affective bonds. At first, he had to step warily, establishing precedents and getting to know people, most of whom, by the very nature of things, felt diffidently toward their royal Chairman. Some time was needed to build confidence and that intimate mutual understanding necessary for sure-footed management. To build the whole group around the person of the Prince was deemed a masterstroke on the part of Retinger.

"Prince Bernhard had great qualities of heart and mind," Healey recalled, "whose harmonious blend results in an enormous personal charm which few people can resist. Also his position is unique. As a royal prince he naturally takes precedence without arousing anybody's envy. He is politically impartial, while the fact that he represents a small country is also reassuring. There were also many intangible but very real and very great advantages in having a royal prince as Chairman."

According to Alden Hatch's 1962 *H. R. H. Prince Bernhard of the Netherlands: An Authorized Biography*, Prince Bernhard, who was chairman, said, "The [first] meeting was most encouraging because people accepted the idea that there would be no publicity, and everybody could speak for himself, irrespective of his position, quite frankly—and fight! It was a beautiful meeting because sparks were flying like crazy between Americans like C. D. Jackson and Britishers like Sir Oliver Franks and Denis Healey and Hugh Gaitskell." Jackson described the initial meeting as follows: "It was all very new and different. We were tucked away in a forest way back in Holland. There were no reporters. Tight security with guards all over the hotel. In the opening hours everyone was uneasy, nervous, sniffing each other like strange dogs. They were afraid to talk very much. Prince Bernhard was everywhere using his charming wiles. People began to thaw. Then they began to fight, which was good. The Prince kept things in hand. When feelings got too tense, he was able to relax people with just the right witty crack, or assert his authority. Though he is so charming, he is made of pretty stern stuff. When he has to restore order he does so in such a way that no one can take offence. But there is no fooling. Order is restored."

A subject of concern to the Europeans was the anti-communist crusade in America led by Wisconsin republican senator Joseph R. McCarthy. Many of them seemed genuinely fearful that the United States was heading for a Fascist dictatorship.

Consequently, on the third day, Bernhard announced, "Even though it is not on the agenda, there has been so much talk of McCarthyism that, if there is time, I am going to ask Mr. Jackson to tell us the American view on that."

An imposing figure, Jackson was well over six feet tall, muscular, with a domed head and a bold, jutting profile. Almost in the manner of a university professor, he told his audience a few facts of political life in the United States. He pointed out that in the American system of government and politics, "We are certain to get this kind of supercharged, emotional freak from time to time. He said that he knew it was hard for Europeans to understand how a Senator of the President's own party could say things on the floor of the Senate completely at variance with the Government's policy." But, he pointed out, there was no way to stop a United States Senator when he went on a rampage.... "Therefore," Jackson said, "the Europeans were right to be interested in this peculiar phenomenon of Senator McCarthy, but wrong to be fearful that he was the first step towards Fascism. Whether McCarthy dies by an assassin's

bullet," he said, "or is eliminated in the normal American way of getting rid of boils on the body politic, I prophesy that by the time we
hold our next meeting he will be gone from the American scene.

"The first Bilderberg conference was such a success in promoting
real understanding across the Atlantic that its sponsors decided to con-
tinue the meetings. A permanent Steering Committee was set up to
plan the agenda for future meetings and decide whom to invite according to the subjects to be discussed. Retinger became permanent secretary. . . . Joseph E. Johnson became the first Secretary on the American
side. Otherwise the organization was kept as loose as possible to allow
maximum flexibility. To insure this, the Steering Committee was to have
a membership turnover of new faces at each meeting. . . . Combined
with this was the unwritten rule that anybody who had ever been to a
Bilderberg conference should be able to feel that he could, in a private
capacity, call on any former member he had met. To this end a list of
names and addresses was maintained to which all participants had access. This made possible an expanding continuation of association for
people who might not otherwise have met.

"Three days at a Bilderberg Conference are not only a stimulating
but also an extremely exhausting experience," wrote Bernard's biographer, "especially for Bernhard and the other members of the Steering
Committee."

H. J. Heinz II of the American catsup and relish-making company
described a typical day: "We sit from nine o'clock at the meeting. Right
after lunch we go at it again until seven o'clock. Fifteen minutes to wash
up, and then an executive session of the Steering Committee. That lasts
an hour, and then we have dinner. After that we talk some more, infor-
mally. It's a fifteen-hour day, at least!" Another member of the group
said, "We meet in such beautiful places, but we never have time to look
at the scenery."

The Bilderberg Group agreed to meet once a year, but the Steering
Committee was to meet more frequently. "The regular sessions were

to be attended by from fifty to eighty people. Each meeting would be held in a different country, but follow the same pattern. An entire hotel would be taken over and closely guarded. The members were to live together, eat and drink together, for three days. Wives were not invited." The Bilderberg Group was to be a "brotherhood of friendship and trust."

Expenses of each meeting were to be borne by private subscription in the host country. At the first meeting Bernhard proposed rotating the chairmanship each day, but the members "begged him to become permanent chairman." They felt that "because he was royal and therefore apolitical, and came from a small nation with no large axes to grind, he was, in fact, the logical choice. In addition every one agreed that he handled the meetings extremely well."

Heinz said, "If Prince Bernhard had not existed Retinger would have had to invent him." The prince's biographer noted that there was also the fact that his royalty gave him considerable leverage in inducing these very eminent men to give up their pressing affairs to attend the meetings.

"Retinger brought in many men of the non-Communist but radical left who might not have responded to an invitation from Prince Bernhard. However, even these would probably not have consented to attend a conference with the men of the conservative right had they not been reassured by having in the chair a completely non-political figure."

One participant recorded, "Prince Bernhard in his methodical way prepares very carefully for each meeting by an intensive study of all the subjects on the agenda. Then he takes copious notes at the meetings, and at the end of each session tries to sum up what has been said and perhaps add a few impartial words of his own to clear the air."

Bernhard confessed, "I always go to the meetings with a feeling of great nervousness. There are so many explosive possibilities. But it is always tremendously stimulating and enormously interesting—in fact, great fun. One thing that worries me beforehand is suppose some key person does not show up and the discussions are a flop?"

From Bernhard's point of view, the Bilderberg group afforded him an opportunity to work in private, without violating the parliamentary prohibition against royalty mixing in politics and for the unification of Europe and the Atlantic Community.

"If we could all agree beforehand in principle," said Bernhard, "it would result, without doubt, not in Utopia, but in an extremely strong and healthy Europe. This in turn would bring the United States into the economic community. It would encourage a great deal of free trade throughout the world. Now, the more free trade you have the more difficult you will make it for the new countries of Africa and Asia to set up an autarchy and live in economic isolation, to adopt trade barriers and quotas which after a hundred years or more we are finding out don't pay. From sheer necessity these people will have to join in free trade. And once you get that you can help an underdeveloped country much more easily than if there are a hundred and fifty thousand restrictions. Also it would be easier for them—their national pride—to accept help. That to my mind is the best possible guarantee against Communist influence."

As to Europe, said Bernhard, his dream was economic union. "One thing we need for free exchange of goods," he asserted, "is complete interchangeability of money, a common currency. I'm flat out for that. And this implies a certain political unity. Here comes our greatest difficulty, for the governments of the free nations are elected by the people, and if they do something the people don't like they are thrown out. It is difficult to reeducate people who have been brought up on nationalism to the idea of relinquishing part of their sovereignty to a supranational body. . . . People don't think European enough or Atlantic enough to put the good of all before party politics or national advantage. This is the tragedy. Due to the freedom and democracy we cherish, we aren't able to achieve what we all basically want to do. We don't show the world clearly enough that our way is better than the Communist way, because we quibble and throw bricks at each other's heads. Real unity comes only when we are scared—when the Soviets put the pressure on and the issue is war or not war, though I should not say that because it is so old and sad and obvious. We are moving towards unity, but we crawl like snails when we should run."

• Three •

LOCKED DOORS, CLOSED CURTAINS

"If the Bilderberg Group is not a conspiracy of some sort," wrote C. Gordon Tether of London's *Financial Times* in 1975, "it is conducted in such a way as to give a remarkably good imitation of one."

It has been described as an ultra-VIP international lobby of the power elite of Europe and America, capable of steering international policy from behind closed doors; a capitalist secret society operating entirely through self-interest and plotting world domination; or a harmless discussion group of politicians, academics, and business tycoons gathered in a luxurious place for three pampered days.

In *Asia Times Online*, Pepé Escobar wrote that "the Bilderberg club is regarded by many financial and business elites as the high chamber of the high priests of capitalism. You can't apply for membership of such a club. Each year, a mysterious 'steering committee' devises a selected invitation list with a maximum 100 names. The location of their annual meeting is not exactly secret. They even have a headquarters in Leiden, in the Netherlands. But the meetings are shrouded in the utmost secrecy.

"Participants and guests rarely reveal that they are attending. Their security is managed by military intelligence. But what is the secretive group really up to? They talk. They lobby. They try to magnify their already immense political clout, on both sides of the Atlantic. Everybody pledges absolute secrecy on what has been discussed."

From the beginning, the Group operated under strictures known as the Chatham House Rule. Its origin dates to 1919 when the "British and American delegates to the Paris Peace Conference conceived the idea of an Anglo-American institute of foreign affairs to study international problems with a view to preventing future wars." As a result of this, "the British Institute of International Affairs was founded in London in July 1920 and received its Royal Charter in 1926 to become the Royal Institute of International Affairs" (RIIA). (The Americans created their own such group and named it the Council on Foreign Relations.) In 1927, the RIIA adopted a rule governing use of information revealed in its discussions that was adopted by the Bilderberg Group. It states that "participants are free to use the information received, but neither the identity nor the affiliation of the speaker(s), nor that of any other participant, may be revealed."

After an introductory speaker, the Group proceeds with discussions conducted by panels of speakers on particular subjects. These consist of three members and discussions that last for approximately two hours. With the meeting opened to everyone, any delegate may "speak for one, three or five minutes. They indicate how long they wish to talk by raising one, three or five fingers. One-minute speakers go first." At the outset of the meetings in the mid-1950s, the topics were primarily related to relations between Europe and the United States, the continuance of the Soviet threat, and the international monetary systems. Delegates were restricted to individuals from Europe and North America (U.S. and Canada). Each country was allowed three delegates consisting of a prominent industry or business leader, a high-ranking politician or official in the government, and an "intellectual," such as an academic or notable journalist. Each country had a coordinator who invited participants.

After the first meeting of eighty delegates, the list of invited participants was expanded to one hundred. For the second conference, planners selected the Hotellerie du Bas-Breau in Barbizon, France (March 18–20), with the third meeting held between September 23 and 25 in the same year at the Grand Hotel Sonnenbichl in Garmisch-Partenkirchen, West Germany. In 1956, the Group met in May at the Hotel Store Kro in Fredensborg, Denmark.

The first parting of the Group's secrecy curtain occurred during its first meting in the United States, held between February 15 and 17, 1957, at the King and Prince Hotel on St. Simons Island, Georgia. Under the headline "Spooky Parley on Georgia Island," syndicated columnist Westbrook Pegler wrote, "Something very mysterious is going on when a strange assortment of 67 self-qualified, polyglot designers and arbiters of the economic and political fate of our Western world go into a secret huddle on an island off Brunswick, Ga., and not a word gets into the popular press beyond a little routine AP [Associated Press] story. These gumshoe superstate schemers were drawn from all the NATO countries."

Originally a sportswriter, Pegler became a popular opinion columnist in the 1930s and 1940s. He was the first columnist to receive the Pulitzer Prize in journalism. Famous for his criticisms of President Franklin D. Roosevelt and scathing items about Mrs. Roosevelt, he had been a vigorous supporter of Senator Joseph McCarthy. Noting that he had learned about the St. Simons Island meeting from a reader who had been told that the hotel had been "alive" with Secret Service and FBI agents, Pegler wrote that he had been unable to verify the presence of the government men, but he had learned that among those at the island meeting were the editor of *The Atlanta Journal*, Ralph McGill, and *The New York Times* publisher Arthur Hays Sulzberger.

A few months later, in an item dated April 12, 1957, Pegler found a worrying parallel between the Bilderberg meeting (a name for the group that Pegler did not know) and one that had been held in 1908. Referring to the Bilderberg meeting as the "mysterious congress of

American and European wiseguys" on St. Simons Island in February, he described such a secret conference that was held on nearby Jekyll Island, Georgia, in the spring of 1908 as an "equally presumptuous group of self-acknowledged superintellectuals" that had resulted in the creation of the United States Federal Reserve System.

"The similarity of the secret meeting of 29 years ago," Pegler said, "and the recent whispering session is irresistible."

In October 1957, a report in the London *Sunday Times* noted that "financiers and businessmen from Britain, the United States, Canada and thirteen other Western nations had begun private talks at Fiuggi, Italy, on the European free trade area and the Common Market projects." The item stated that there were sixty delegates at the Grand Hotel Palazzo della Fonte between October 4 and 6 and that "it was a point of honor" that no immediate disclosure be made of the subjects under discussion.

"The whole point," said the Sunday *Times*, "was that members should be able to discuss problems of interest on both sides of the Atlantic without committing their Governments. All the members were speaking as private individuals."

Success of the Bilderberg Group's rule of silence was ensured by two aspects of human nature: the desire to be an "insider" who is entrusted with secrets. The allure of being among the world's elite and allowed to rub elbows, chat at cocktail parties, dine in splendor, and play cards or golf with royalty, prime ministers, presidents, statesmen, millionaires, intellectuals, and celebrity journalists in a five-star hotel guaranteed compliance. "It is not only flattering to be invited again and again, and to believe that your opinion is considered important," said one veteran Bilderberger who spoke only on the guarantee of anonymity, "it's fun."

Another regular attendee in the 1950s who demanded assurance of nonattribution explained, "The Bilderberg Group was the first of the almost countless so-called think tanks that have sprouted everywhere, especially in Washington, DC. If the Chatham House rules had not been adopted, the Group could not have been effective as a freewheeling forum."

A British observer of the Bilderberg Group wrote, "Many of those invited to come along, perhaps to report on matters pertaining to their expertise, have little idea there is a formally constituted group at all, let alone one with its own grand agenda. Hence the rather dismissive remarks by people like sixties media guru Marshall McLuhan, who attended a Bilderberg meeting in 1969 in Denmark, that he was 'nearly suffocated at the banality and irrelevance,' describing them as 'uniformly nineteenth century minds pretending to relate to the twentieth century.' Another of those who attended, Christopher Price [a Labour member of Parliament] found it 'icing on the cake with nothing to do with the cake.' "

From the beginning, Bilderberg was administered by a small core group called a Steering Committee, consisting of a permanent chair, a U.S. chair, European and North American secretaries, and a treasurer. Invitations are sent only to important and generally respected people who through their special knowledge or experience, their personal contacts, and their influence in national and international circles can further the aims set by Bilderberg. Retinger's secretary, John Pomian, said that "during the first three or four years the all-important selection of participants was a delicate and difficult task. This was particularly so as regards politicians," he noted. "It was not easy to persuade the top officeholders to come. . . . Retinger displayed great skill and an uncanny ability to pick out people who in a few years time were to accede to the highest offices in their respective countries. . . . Today there are very few figures among governments on both sides of the Atlantic who have not attended at least one of these meetings."

Bilderberg discussions are organized on the principle of reaching consensus rather than through formal resolutions and voting.

In September 1958, the meeting took place in Buxton, England. It was said that with the exception of three very old residents, the Palace Hotel at Buxton was cleared of guests, and the usual hotel staff was temporarily suspended and replaced by staffs brought in by attendees. Among them were John J. McCloy and David Rockefeller of the Chase Manhattan bank; Paul Rykens, a Dutch banker and member of the Anglo-Dutch Trade Council; former U.S. secretary of state Dean Acheson; Eisenhower aide Gabriel Hauge; Denis Healey; H. J. Heinz; future U.S. arms negotiator Paul H. Nitze; British diplomat David Ormsby-Gore; and several industrialists and financiers from the Netherlands, Greece, Belgium, and Germany.

After meeting in Istanbul, Turkey, in September 1959, the Group returned to Europe for its next conference (Nidwalden, Switzerland) in May 1960. A month later, they learned of the death of Joseph Retinger (June 12, 1960). Replacing him as secretary was E. H. van der Beugel of the Netherlands, who had headed the Dutch bureau of the Marshall Plan.

Returning to the United States in 1964, the Group convened in historic Williamsburg, Virginia, from March 20 to 22. In the twenty years since its founding, the nature of the attendees reflected the two decades of changes in the world. Those who attended the 1954 conference met in the shadow of a Soviet threat that had required the free nations of Europe to seek shelter under the umbrella of NATO with the assurance that American military power would hold the Soviets at bay. With Communism checked, an increasingly frequent topic of discussion among Group members was proposals for political and economic unification of Europe.

"Fresh in the minds of many Bilderbergers was a statement by President John F. Kennedy that in just twenty years one man, Jean Monnet, had done more to unite Europe than a thousand years of conquerors. Monnet's vision transformed a whole continent and forged an entirely new form of political governance."

Monnet did so without being elected to office.

Born in 1888, the son of a cognac dealer, he was a lifelong socialist. At the age of sixteen, he abandoned formal education and moved to London. He spent two years learning business and English. In 1906, his father sent him abroad to work for the family business. He made numerous trips to Scandinavia, Russia, Egypt, Canada, and the United States. Although excused from military service in 1914 for health reasons, he still wanted to be helpful and proposed a plan that would coordinate the Allies' war resources that the French government agreed should be implemented.

Success at coordinating supplies during World War I led to Monnet's nomination, at the age of thirty-one, as deputy secretary-general of the newly formed League of Nations. It was at the meeting of the victors in the Great War at Versailles, that Monnet and Joseph Retinger met. Although Monnet's memoirs did not mention encountering Retinger, it is reasonable to assume that they discussed their mutual vision of a unified Europe. But it was Monnet to whom history awarded the title "Founding Father of the European Union."

He resigned from the League in 1923 in order to devote himself to managing the family business. As an international financier, he was instrumental in the economic recovery of several Central and Eastern European nations, helping to stabilize the currency of Poland and Romania. "In 1929, his experience in international finance led him to found and co-manage Bancamerica-Blair, a large U.S. bank in San Francisco. From 1934 to 1936, at the invitation of President Chiang Kai-shek, he lived in China, assisting with the reorganization of the Chinese railway network. Commissioned in 1938 to negotiate an order for French military aircraft from the United States, he was sent to London in December 1939 by the French and British governments to oversee collectivization of the countries' production capacities."

After France was invaded and defeated by Germany in June 1940, Monnet was sent to the United States by the British government as a member of the British Supply Council, in order to negotiate the purchase of war supplies. In meetings with President Roosevelt, he discussed the urgent need of Britain and France for military assistance in the form of a "Victory Program" that would sustain them until U.S. entry into the war. Until that occurred, the United States was to be what Roosevelt in a famous radio address called "the arsenal of democracy" by providing arms to the British and French.

Primary responsibility for overseeing this fell on the shoulders of Roosevelt's military advisor, U.S. Army chief of staff George Catlett Marshall. When the U.S. was drawn into the war by the Japanese sneak attack on Pearl Harbor, Marshall led no troops into battle, but he possessed a unique gift for finding bold commanders, a genius for devising strategy, a brilliance in planning, and the skills needed to build armed forces capable of waging a two-front world war and mobilizing American industry to provide everything required to win it.

When *Time* magazine named him Man of the Year in 1943, it said, "Hired by the U.S. people to do a job, he will be as good, as ruthless, as tough, as this job requires. There his ambitions stop. He shuns all avoidable publicity, he is a man of great personal reserve, but the U.S. people have learned why they trust General Marshall more than they have trusted any military man since George Washington: he is a civis Americanus."

From an army of 200,000 men when he became Army chief of staff on the day Hitler's Germany invaded Poland to begin the second world war, he built the largest military in U.S. history and developed the plan to wage a two-front war against Germany and Japan. During the years before the war, he had recognized, gotten to know, and remembered men with leadership qualities: Dwight D. Eisenhower, Omar Bradley, George Patton, Mark Clark, Lucian Truscott, J. Lawton (Joe) Collins, and others who became commanders of ground forces in Europe and the Pacific. As Army chief of staff, Marshall possessed organizational skills that converted an army of only several hundred thousand, with few modern weapons and no modern battle experience, into a force of more than eight million. During the war, he attended meetings between President Roosevelt and Winston Churchill from the conference on the Atlantic Charter to Casablanca (1943), Quebec (1943), Cairo and Teheran (1943), with them and Stalin at Yalta in 1945, and with Truman, Churchill, and Stalin at Potsdam (1945).

In 1947 as secretary of state, Marshall proposed a plan for European economic recovery that came to bear his name. In response to Marshall's speech, sixteen European nations agreed to attend a conference in Paris on July 12, 1947, to form the Committee for European Economic Cooperation (CEEC). Its chairman was a British civil servant, Oliver Franks, but the key figure was his vice chairman, Jean Monnet, aided by former Washington lawyer George Ball. Later a Bilderberger, he had come to Paris in August to work for Monnet as an advisor on how the CEEC case for economic aid could most effectively be presented to Washington. The result of their work was a report that said in "the period 1948–1951, the sixteen nations would need $19.1 billion. Seven days later, on December, 19, 1947, after making provision for emergency aid to France, Italy and Austria, President Truman submitted to Congress a 'European Recovery Bill,' requesting $17 billion over four years.

"Revisionist historians contend that while the Marshall Plan has generally been viewed as an altruistic gesture by the United States to help impoverished allies in their hour, underlying it were commercial interests.... Economic support for Europe represented an opportunity to find outlets for American products." An even more significant element in the Marshall Plan, stated one critic, was that despite an apparent "hands off" approach politically, the conditions imposed on recipient countries were designed to promote a federal Europe.

Desire for a European Union was voiced by Winston Churchill. On May 14, 1947, in a speech at London's Albert Hall, he launched an "all-party United Europe Movement," with his son-in-law, Duncan Sandys [member of Parliament and future Bilderberger], as president of a committee that included two members of the Labour cabinet and several future conservative cabinet ministers. Churchill called for a "United States of Europe," of which the United States, the Soviet Union, and Britain could be sponsors, that advocated reintegration of Germany into the Western world.

With the defeat of Germany, Monnet had feared that a return to business as usual would see Europe fall back into its historical cycle of conflict and war. As tensions grew between the French and Germany over Germany's industrial Ruhr region, he proposed the pooling of Franco-German coal and steel resources under a supranational high authority. As the head of France's General Planning Commission, he was the author of what came to be known as the "Schuman Plan," to create the European Coal and Steel Community (ECSC).

Described by Merry and Serge Bromberger in their biography of Monnet as "an idea of revolutionary daring," the proposal was welcomed by the French foreign minister, Robert Schuman and German chancellor Konrad Adenauer. Historians recorded this as the seed from which the EU sprang. The result of Franco-German conciliation, Monnet hoped, would eventually be a union of European nations with a single market, single currency, and common foreign policy.

"Europe will not be conjured up in a stroke, nor by an overall design," he said. "It will be attained by concrete achievements generating an active community of interest."

"Once the ECSC was established," wrote William F. Jasper in a sharply critical essay in *The New American* in 2004, "Monnet was named the first president of this powerful cartel that controlled the production of energy and steel for much of continental Europe." In 1955, Monnet founded the Action Committee for a United States of Europe. A result of its efforts was the 1957 Treaty of Rome, which created the

European Common Market. One of the "Founding Fathers" of the EU, Robert Schuman was born in Luxembourg in 1886, but grew up in France. In 1919, he was elected a deputy to the French Parliament, where he served for twenty years. Following World War II, he served as France's prime minister and as foreign minister and finance minister. From 1955 to 1961, he was president of the European Movement, and from 1958 to 1960 was president of the European Parliament in Strasbourg.

Critics of the European Movement, and those who detect a conspiracy in the Bilderberg Group, have asserted that they were almost completely financed with funds provided by the CIA, the Marshall Plan, and nongovernmental sources such as the Ford, Rockefeller, and Carnegie foundations.

Another figure in realizing European unification was Paul-Henri Spaak (1899–1972). Known as "Mr. Socialist," he was elected to Belgium's parliament as a member of the Labour Party in 1932 and later served several times as Belgium's foreign minister and four times as prime minister. He also presided over the Consultative Assembly of the Council of Europe and the General Assembly of the ECSC in the early days of both organizations. In 1945, he was the first elected chairman of the UN General Assembly.

In 1948, he accompanied Winston Churchill, Duncan Sandys, and Joseph Retinger on a trip to America that was said to be an effort to secure U.S. funding for the European Movement. The result was formation of the American Committee for a United Europe, headed by William Donovan, former director of the OSS, and Allen Dulles, future CIA director. In 1955 Spaak chaired a preparatory committee for a Conference of European leaders in Messina, Sicily.

In the Messina agreement of 1955, representatives of the governments of the Federal Republic of Germany, Belgium, France, Italy, Luxembourg, and the Netherlands stated that the time had come to take "a new step on the road of European construction" through establishment of a united Europe that "must be achieved through the development of common institutions, the progressive fusion of national economies, the creation of a common market, and the gradual harmonization of their social policies."

The representatives declared that this was indispensable "if Europe is to preserve the standing which she has in the world, to restore the influence and her prestige, and to improve steadily the living standard of the population."

A second step in the direction of a unified Europe occurred in 1957. Signed on March 25, the Treaties of Rome created the European Atomic Energy Community and the European Economic Community (EEC), or "Common Market." In this entity, the "inner six" nations were Belgium, West Germany, Luxembourg, France, Italy, and the Netherlands. The "outer seven" nations of the Organization for European Economic Cooperation (OEEC) that did not join the Common Market were the United Kingdom, Norway, Sweden, Denmark, Austria, Switzerland, and Portugal. Explaining why Britain did not join the Common Market, Foreign Minister Ernest Bevin said, "If you open that Pandora's box, you never know what Trojan horses will jump out."

As a result of these developments, the subject of European unity found its way into Bilderberg discussions, but the participants in the 1960s were increasingly younger men for whom the problems that were debated by the Group in the 1950s were history. The threat from the Soviet Union was no longer that Europe might be overrun by tanks of the Red Army, but intercontinental nuclear missiles. In a military standoff known as Mutual Assured Destruction, the contest with the Soviets had become a test between communism and capitalism.

Although world economics always had a place on the Bilderberg agenda, the subject became increasingly important as the "first world" governments of Europe and the United States found themselves facing attempts by the Soviet Union to gain influence in the "third world" nations of Asia, Africa, and oil-rich countries of the Middle East. The world supply of oil that was the basis of the global economy rocketed to the top of the Group's agenda for the April 1974 meeting in Megeve, France, because the Arab-Israeli (Six Days') War of 1973 had resulted in an embargo by the Arab oil-producing countries (OPEC), creating a worldwide economic crisis. Reflecting this sudden attention to the Middle East, the 1975 meeting was held in the city of Izmir in Turkey.

In 1976, the Group was shaken by a revelation that Bernhard had received bribes totaling over a million dollars from U.S. aircraft manufacturer Lockheed, in his capacity as the inspector general of the Dutch armed forces. After an investigation determined he had solicited bribes from the U.S. plane manufacturer to influence the Dutch government's purchase of fighter aircraft, he relinquished his military titles, all his public offices, and his role as the Bilderberg Group's chief motivating force and host. Plans to hold the 1976 Group meeting in Hot Springs, Virginia, in April were canceled.

Describing the most important figure in founding of the Bilderberg Group, Alden Hatch wrote in *H. R. H. Prince Bernhard of the Netherlands* that Bernhard in his methodical way prepared very carefully for each meeting by an intensive study of all the subjects on the agenda. As mentioned previously, not only did he take copious notes at the meetings, but at the end of each session he prepared a summary of what had been said, sometimes adding some comments, which he hoped were fairly objective.

In spite of the preliminary work, Prince Bernhard, as we saw, always felt very nervous going to the meetings. With such a range of possibilities, it was still "tremendously stimulating and enormously interesting—in fact, great fun." Despite a recurrent worry that one or more important people might not attend, making the meeting "a flop," he reported that in fact such a thing had seldom happened.

The rule of the meetings was that each man was allowed five minutes to talk, and at the end of this time the prince was allowed five minutes to talk, and at the end of this time the prince began to make signals to the speaker to stop.

"Once or twice I've had to be unpleasant to somebody, but that is very difficult for me," the prince told Hatch. "It is also difficult to keep a big boy from talking too long. I swing my wristwatch in front of his face and say, 'Ah, ah, more than five minutes!' And if somebody makes a really short speech I say, 'Now that is wonderful.' The shorter the speech the more it sticks in our minds. But that does not always help, you know. Some people are very difficult."

The only meeting, other than the first, at which Bernhard did not preside all the way through was in Switzerland in 1960. He arrived with a bad cold. After presiding at the opening session he developed viral pneumonia.

"The Bilderberg meetings were never dull," Hatch wrote. "Even though the group was . . . 'like belonging to a fraternity, sparks flew at nearly every one. At St. Simons Island in 1957, the French, British, and Americans almost came to blows over the Suez Canal crisis of 1956. At another it was the issue of the Chinese islands of Quemoy and Matsu.

Other hot issues while Bernhard presided were the European Common Market and the British and American attitudes toward it."

"Any attempt to evaluate the effect of the Bilderberg Group was nearly impossible because of the nature and object of the conferences, which was not to act or even to convince, but rather to enlighten. Prince Bernhard said, 'You are not asked to agree, merely to listen.' "

United States under secretary of state George W. Ball said, "I think the most useful feature of the Bilderberg meetings is the opportunity for responsible people in industry, statecraft, or politics to have a frank discussion where they will not be publicly quoted and are able to give their personal views without their remarks being considered official.

This is unique and without parallel. The character of the meetings has been shaped by the very devoted and astute leadership of Bernhard himself. Without his special position, intelligence, and goodwill nothing like this could come about."

With Bernhard's resignation, the Bilderberg Group entered a new phase.

Four

THE BANKER AND THE BRAIN

When Joseph Retinger proposed the idea of organizing a conference of world leaders to discuss strategies to deal with the problems facing the nations of NATO, high on the list of names on Bernhard's invitation roster was David Rockefeller.

Born in 1915, the youngest son of multimillionaire John D. Rockefeller, Jr., David had attended school in New York City and graduated with a bachelor's degree in English history and literature from Harvard University in 1936. This was followed with a Ph.D. in economics from the University of Chicago and a further study at both Harvard and the London School of Economics. Along with his brothers, John D. III, Nelson, Laurance, and Winthrop, he established the Rockefeller Brothers Fund in 1940. Secretary to New York City Mayor Fiorello H. LaGuardia (1940–1941), he was also assistant regional director of the United States Office of Defense, Health and Welfare Service (1941–1942). Enlisted in the U.S. Army in 1942, he served as a military intelligence officer in North Africa and Southern France and set up an intelligence network in Algiers.

After serving as an assistant military attaché in Paris in the last seven months of the war, he returned home and joined the Chase National (merged in 1955 to become the Chase Manhattan Bank) Bank as an assistant manager. Later, as senior vice president of Chase National Bank he had the responsibility for supervising the economic research department and customer relations in the metropolitan New York region, including all the New York City branches.

Invited by Prince Bernhard to attend the first Bilderberg meeting in 1954, he became one of its founders and a member of the Steering Committee. Following Bernard's resignation, he assumed effective direction of the Group and emerged on the world stage as a proponent of American internationalism. Referring to this in his memoirs, he wrote, "For more than a century, ideological extremists at either end of the political spectrum have seized upon well-publicized incidents to attack the Rockefeller family for the inordinate influence they claim we wield over American political and economic institutions. Some even believe we are part of a secret cabal working against the best interests of the United States, characterizing my family and me as 'internationalists' and of conspiring with others around the world to build a more integrated global political and economic structure—one world, if you will. If that's the charge, I stand guilty and I am proud of it."

In a lengthy article in *The New York Times* at the time of the publication of Rockefeller's *Memoirs* in 2002, David Brooks, senior editor at *The Weekly Standard* and contributing editor at *Newsweek*, provided not only a portrait of David Rockefeller but one of the rare references found in the *Times* of the Bilderberg Group. (In a search of more than 120 years of the paper's archives, the term "Bilderberg Group" appeared less than a dozen times, with little or no explanation of its history and purpose.) Noting only that Rockefeller was "there at the creation" of the Group, Brooks wrote that "he positively excelled at the sober sort of networking that is appreciated in the executive suites where the wood paneling is dark and the cuff links are subtle." Describing him as "a Mozart of modulated tones," Brooks observed, "He is never furious, though he is occasionally 'distressed.' An event is never horrible, it is 'disagreeable.' "

Referring to Rockefeller's participation in forums such as Bilderberg meetings, Brooks quipped, "His ability to endure tedium must be unmatched in all human history."

The only representative of the United States to rival Rockefeller in influence in the Bilderberg Group was a Rockefeller protégé.

Born in Furth, Germany, on May 27, 1923, Henry Kissinger fled the Nazis with his family in 1938 and went first to England and then to the United States. They settled in New York, where Kissinger completed high school and took night classes at City College with the intention of becoming an accountant. While in college he worked at a factory during the day. During World War II, he joined the military and served in Army Intelligence in Germany. He also became an American citizen. Following the war, he stayed in Europe as an instructor at the European Command Intelligence School in Germany. In 1947 he returned to the United States and enrolled at Harvard University and graduated in the class of 1950 with a degree in government. He continued his studies as a graduate student, earning a master's degree in 1952 and a Ph.D. in 1954, while also teaching at the university. Between 1952 and 1969, he directed the Harvard International Seminar, a type of study in which advanced students, led by a professor, conducted research, shared their findings, and contributed to discussions. As part of the Council on Foreign Relations (founded by Rockefeller), he added to his reputation as an expert on international relations and national defense policy.

For eighteen months beginning in 1956, he was director of a Rockefeller Brothers Fund special studies project that was developed to investigate possible domestic and international problems. In 1957 he became a lecturer at Harvard and was promoted to professor in 1962. He also served as a consultant to the National Security Council, the Arms Control Disarmament Agency, and the Rand Corporation. From 1962 to 1965, he worked full-time at Harvard and in 1965 he became a consultant to the State Department on Vietnam and visited the country several times between 1965 and 1967.

For most of 1968, he worked on the unsuccessful bid of New York governor Nelson Rockefeller (David's older brother) for the Republican presidential nomination. Despite his loss to Richard Nixon, Rockefeller urged Nixon to appoint Kissinger to head the National Security Council. Some Bilderberg observers claim that it was on orders from the Group that Kissinger engineered President Richard Nixon's secret visit to Red China for a summit meeting with Chou En-Lai, the Chinese Premier. Traveling secretly to China in July 1971, Kissinger made the arrangements. The result was a 1972 meeting between Nixon, Chou, and Communist Party chairman Mao Tse Dong, that formalized relations between the two countries, ending twenty-three years of diplomatic isolation and mutual hostility. The historic conference created a tacit strategic anti-Soviet alliance between China and the United States.

While Kissinger's diplomacy led to economic and cultural exchanges between the two sides and the establishment of liaison offices in the Chinese and American capitals that the Bilderberg Group welcomed, the success was soon overshadowed by the Watergate scandal that some Bilderberg critics believe was also a result of a Bilderberg plot to "oust Nixon because Nixon publically declared he did not approve of the General Agreement on Tariffs and Trade (GATT)."

As a leading proponent of this fanciful scenario, Daniel Estulin wrote in *The True Story of the Bilderberg Group*, "Disgracing Nixon and drumming him out of office handed Kissinger unprecedented power the likes of which have never been seen since. With Nixon's resignation, the Bilderbergers finally saw 'their' president, Gerald Ford, move into the White House."

President Ford would take "direct orders from Henry Kissinger, an agent of David Rockefeller, a servant of the Bilderbergers."

When Nixon elevated Kissinger to secretary of state, Kissinger's work in attaining an end to the war in Vietnam would earn Kissinger the Nobel Peace Prize.

In the years since Bernhard withdrew from the Group, no Americans would be more influential regarding the direction of Bilderberg conferences than David Rockefeller, and no member of the Bilderberg Group would attract more world attention and controversy than Kissinger. While Rockefeller showed that he was the Mozart of modulated tones depicted by David Brooks, Kissinger revealed that there were limits to his reputation as the diplomat who had kept his cool in negotiations with the North Vietnamese Communists.

When Olaf Palme, Swedish prime minister, issued a scorching attack on the United States for its bombings in Vietnam and quietly sent word through diplomatic channels that Kissinger would not be welcome in Sweden for the 1973 Bilderberg meeting, Kissinger's State Department objected and leaked the Swedish objection to Kissinger to the press.

When Bernhard learned of this and threatened to move the Bilderberg meeting elsewhere, the prime minister said there had been a misunderstanding and Kissinger would certainly be a welcome guest at the palatial Grand Hotel in the city of Saltsjöbaden.

Much of the discussion time was devoted to increasing demands on the world's supply of oil and the dependence of Europe and North America on a low price and its continual flow. The American view was that the energy problem was compounded by the continued requests for price increases by the Middle East producers, the threat to the availability of supplies, and the use of oil for political purposes. As the Bilderbergers met in the following April at the Mont d'Arbois in Megeve, France, the American worries had become a reality.

Reeling from a humiliating defeat by Israel in a conflict in October 1973, known as the Six Days' War, in which Kissinger invented "shuttle diplomacy" in an effort to end it, the primarily Arab oil-producing nations (OAPEC, Syria, and Egypt) imposed a crippling oil embargo that cut off shipments to the West.

Because the subject of oil was the predominant topic of the 1973

Bilderberg meeting, suspicions arose that the bankers, oil corporation executives, and politicians in the Group had conspired to foster the oil embargo crisis in order to profit from it. Helping to stoke these suspicions were several freelance journalists, libertarian publications, and "conspiracy theorists" who found in the Group's elite membership and the secrecy of its meetings a sinister plot to gain control of world affairs.

In *The True Story of the Bilderbeg Group*, Daniel Estulin wrote, "Since 1954, the Bilderbergers have represented the elite and the absolute wealth of all Western nations, financiers, industrialists, bankers, politicians, business leaders or multinational corporations, presidents, prime ministers, finance ministers, state secretaries, World Bank and International Monetary Fund representatives, presidents of world media conglomerates, and military leaders."

They meet, says British journalist and regular Bilderberg observer Tony Gosling, with the purpose of running the world. "When such rich and powerful people meet up in secret," he wrote, "with military intelligence managing their security, with hardly a whisper escaping of what goes on inside, people are right to be suspicious. But the true power of Bilderberg comes from the fact that participants are in a bubble, sealed off from reality."

Describing the Group as an extremely influential lobbying group, Gosling believed that the Bilderberger organizers' hidden agenda was to accumulate wealth and power into their own hands through "globalization." The ideology put forward at the annual conferences was that "what's good for banking and big business is good for the mere mortals of the world."

Five

THE BILDERBERG PLAN FOR CONTROLLING THE WORLD

At the forty-eighth Bilderberg meeting, held in Brussels, Belgium, from June 1 to 3, 2000, subjects included the U.S. elections, globalization, the Balkans, and the expansion of the EU. The press release stated, "What is unique about Bilderberg as a forum is the broad cross section of leading citizens that are assembled for informal and off-the-record discussion about topics of current concern especially in the fields of foreign affairs and the international economy; the strong feeling among participants that in view of the differing attitudes and experiences of the Western nations, there remains a clear need to further develop an understanding in which these concerns can be accommodated; and the privacy of the meetings, which has no purpose other than to allow participants to speak their minds openly and freely. In short Bilderberg is a small, flexible, informal, and off-the-record international forum in which different viewpoints can be expressed and mutual understanding enhanced."

When asked by an interviewer of the BBC if the Bilderberg Group consisted of a global ruling class, Viscount Etienne Davignon of Belgium, the Group chairman, replied, "I simply think it's people who have influence interested to speak to other people who have influence."

At age seventy-three, an avuncular, pipe-smoking veteran of the Belgian ministry of foreign affairs who had been responsible for the Political Department of the Ministry until his departure in 1977 for the European Commission, Davignon was also a key figure in preparing a report on the future of the Atlantic Alliance and had presided over a committee that prepared the first proposals regarding political cooperation between members of the EEC. Following the oil crisis in 1973, he chaired an international conference that established an oil-sharing treaty. From 1974 to 1977, he served as the first president of the International Energy Agency. In 1991, he became chairman of the Association for the Monetary Union of Europe. As a member of the European Roundtable of Industrialists, he chaired a working group on trade and investment. He was also a distinguished member of the Dutch Royal Institute for International Relations.

In the rare BBC interview, conducted in his lavish office in the Brussels headquarters of a conglomerate that managed the Suez Canal, Davignon said, "Bilderberg does not try to reach conclusions. It does not try to say 'what we should do.' Everyone goes away with their own feeling and that allows the debate to be open and frank and to see what the differences are. Business influences society and politics influences society. That's purely common sense. It's not that business contests the right of democratically elected leaders to lead."

Asked what was the point of Bilderberg in a chaotic world, Davignon answered, "To be as useful as one can. It's a modest agenda."

Queried if the Group ever reached general agreement on issues, he said, "Not really. The problems we deal with are of a general nature and don't adjust to simple answers. What can come out is that it's not wrong to try to deal with a problem and that you should go home and encourage people not to leave the problem on the table. But a real consensus, an action plan? The answer is no. People are much too sensible to believe they can do that."

About deciding what was discussed and who was invited to attend Bilderberg meetings, Davignon said, "There are no permanent members, but a small steering committee tries to decide issues of joint interest to Europeans and Americans. And we have to have enough people who have never been to Bilderberg before so you keep a momentum and not simply have an old boys' club, and there are enough people who have been before who understand the format: that you speak shortly, you speak your mind, and that nothing will ever be quoted. You also try to look at people who would be interested (in attending) in relation to their own ambition to share thoughts with others. And then, by happy accident, you invite people who go to great places, but then you also invite people who go nowhere."

Said Bilderberg founder Denis Healey, "To say we were striving for a one-world government is exaggerated. Those of us in Bilderberg felt we couldn't go on forever fighting one another for nothing and killing people and rendering millions homeless. So we felt that a single community throughout the world would be a good thing. Bilderberg is a way of bringing together politicians, industrialists, financiers, and journalists. We make a point of helping along younger politicians who are obviously rising, to bring them together with financiers and industrialists who offer them wise words. It increases the chance of having a sensible global policy."

While these explanations of the purpose and goals of the Bilderberg Group may seem to be benign to the average citizen of Europe or the United States, the secrecy surrounding it since its inception in 1954 has aroused suspicions that the true objective is the creation of a world government controlled by a wealthy elite and officials of global corporations with the goal of establishing a New World Order in which the ruling elite would impose:

- A single international identity
- Centralized political control
- A world bank
- A global currency
- Centralized control of education

- One legal system with a world court
- An international police force (NATO)
- Worldwide free trade.

Achievement of these goals would be in stages, beginning with a European Union and followed by a merging of the United States, Canada, and Mexico into a single entity; a South and Central American federation; and an Asian-Pacific union. These would eventually be melded into a world government controlled by an elite group of bankers, industrialists, and intellectuals. All of this would be accomplished by introducing the concept of "globalization" as inevitable and beneficial. National identification was to become subservient to internationalism. World peace would be ensured by an international military force based on an expanded NATO. All of this would be given the appearance of democracy, but power would be vested in the hands of an unelected elite. Having been stymied by the existence of the Soviet Union and its announced policy of spreading Communism throughout the world, the Bilderberg Group also struggled to attain its initial goal of creating the EU that had been Joseph Retinger's dream. But with the collapse of the Soviet Union and the discrediting of communism/socialism, the way seemed to be clear for European unification.

As a European Union appeared to be within reach, only Great Britain stood in the way. While the nations of the continent fell into line by joining the European federation, eliminating passports, and adopting a common currency (the Euro), the British steadfastly resisted by clinging to the pound and refusing to surrender national sovereignty.

Eventually, even the British were drawn into the EU, but not without continuing objections.

As mentioned earlier, in the drive to create a European Union that began with adoption of the Treaty of Rome to build an EEC on March 25, 1957, the goal was creation of a common market covering a whole range of goods and services. Customs duties between the six-member countries were completely abolished on July 1, 1968. "So successful was this venture," noted an EU historian, "that Denmark, Ireland, and the United Kingdom decided to join the Community." This first enlargement, "from six to nine members, took place in 1973. At the same time, new social and environmental policies were implemented, and the European Regional Development Fund (ERDF) was established in 1975.

"On June 4, 1979, a decisive step forward for the European Community was taken with the first elections to the European Parliament by direct universal suffrage. In 1981, Greece joined the Community, followed by Spain and Portugal in 1986. This strengthened the European Economic Union's presence in southern Europe. Although a worldwide economic recession in the early 1980s brought with it a wave of "euro-pessimism," in 1985 the European Commission, under its president Jacques Delors, published a White Paper setting out a timetable for completing the European single market by January 1, 1993. This ambitious goal was enshrined in the Single European Act, which was signed in February 1986 and came into force on July 1, 1987.

"The political shape of Europe was dramatically altered when the Berlin Wall fell in 1989. This led to the unification of Germany in October 1990 and the coming of democracy to the countries of central and eastern Europe as they broke away from Soviet control. The Soviet Union itself ceased to exist in December 1991. At the same time, the member states were negotiating the new Treaty on European Union, which was adopted by the European Council, composed of presidents or prime ministers or both, in Maastricht, the Netherlands, in December 1991. The Treaty came into force on November 1, 1993. By adding areas of intergovernmental cooperation to existing integrated Community structures, the Treaty created the European Union."

A strategy for modernizing the European economy and enabling it to compete on the world market with other major players such as the United States and the newly industrialized countries involved encouraging innovation and business investment and adapting Europe's education systems to meet the needs of the information society.

"In the mid-1990s, the former Soviet-bloc countries (Bulgaria, the Czech Republic, Hungary, Poland, Romania and Slovakia), the three Baltic states that had been part of the Soviet Union (Estonia, Latvia and Lithuania), one of the republics of former Yugoslavia (Slovenia), and two Mediterranean countries (Cyprus and Malta) all began knocking at the EU's door. Negotiations on future membership opened in December 1997. The EU enlargement to 25 countries took place on May 1, 2004, when 10 of the 12 candidates joined. Bulgaria and Romania followed on January 1, 2007," according to one source.

"At the European Council in Madrid in June 1989, EU leaders adopted a three-stage plan for economic and monetary union. This plan became part of the Maastricht Treaty on European Union adopted by the European Council in December 1991." Under the Economic and Monetary Union (EMU), the aims were "free movement of capital within the EU by abolition of exchange controls; increasing the amount of resources devoted to removing inequalities between European regions (Structural Funds); economic convergence, through multilateral surveillance of member states' economic policies; establishing the European Monetary Institute (EMI) in Frankfurt that was made up of the governors of the central banks of the EU countries; independence of national central banks; and rules to curb national budget deficits."

On January 1, 1999, the Euro became the common currency of Austria, Belgium, Finland, France, Germany, Ireland, Italy, Luxembourg, the Netherlands, Portugal, and Spain. (Greece joined them on January 1, 2001.) At this point, "the European Central Bank took over from the EMI and became responsible for monetary policy, which was defined and implemented in the Euro. Its notes and coins were issued on January 1, 2002, in twelve Euro-area countries. National currencies were withdrawn from circulation two months later. Since then, only the Euro was legal tender for all cash and bank transactions in the euro-area countries, which represented more than two thirds of the EU population.

"The first right of a European citizen in this new structure is the right to travel, work, and live anywhere in the Union. The Treaty of Maastricht enshrined this right in its chapter on citizenship. The EU has passed a directive establishing a system of mutual recognition of higher education qualifications. This directive applies to all university courses lasting three years or more and is based on the principle of mutual confidence in the quality of national education and training systems. Any person who is a national of an EU country can work in health, education, and other public services anywhere in the Union, with the exception of activities covered by the prerogative of public authorities (police, armed forces, foreign affairs, etc.).

"Since 2004, European citizens who travel within the EU could obtain a European health insurance card from their national authorities which helped cover medical costs if they fall ill while in another country. Europeans are considered not just consumers or participants in the economic and social affairs. They are also citizens of the European Union, and as such have specific political rights. Under the Maastricht Treaty, every citizen of the Union, regardless of nationality, has the right to vote and to stand as a candidate in local elections in his or her country of residence and in elections to the European Parliament. . . . Citizenship of the Union is now enshrined in the Treaty which states that 'Every person holding the nationality of a Member State shall be a citizen of the Union. Citizenship of the Union is to complement and not replace national citizenship.' The Treaty of Amsterdam, which came into force in 1999, strengthened the concept of fundamental rights. It introduced a procedure for taking action against an EU country that violates its citizens' fundamental rights. It also extended the principle of nondiscrimination so that it covers not only nationality but also gender, race, religion, age, and sexual orientation."

The EU's commitment to citizens' rights was reaffirmed in Nice,

France, in December 2000 with the solemn proclamation of the Charter of Fundamental Rights of the European Union. This Charter was drawn up by a convention composed of members of national parliaments, representatives of governments, and a member of the European Commission. Under six headings (Dignity, Freedoms, Equality, Solidarity, Citizens' Rights, and Justice), fifty-four articles set out the EU's fundamental values and the civil, political, economic, and social rights of EU citizens. Citizens are given social and economic rights, including the right to strike, the right of workers to be informed and consulted, the right to reconcile family life and professional life, the right to healthcare, social security and social assistance throughout the European Union. The Charter also promotes equality between men and women and introduces rights such as data protection, a ban on eugenic practices, and the reproductive cloning of human beings, the right to environmental protection, the rights of children and elderly people, and the right to good administration.

An Internet website dedicated to the promulgation of the EU declares, "A day will come when all the nations of this continent, without losing their distinct qualities or their glorious individuality, will fuse together in a higher unity to form a European brotherhood. A day will come when the only battlefield will be the marketplace for competing ideas. A day will come when bullets and bombs will be replaced by votes."

The EU calls itself "a pact between sovereign nations which have resolved to share a common destiny and to pool an increasing share of their sovereignty" in a world in which a technological revolution is radically transforming life in the industrialized world. In this "new world," say proponents of globalization, it is vital to understand that new challenges transcend traditional frontiers. Sustainable development, world population trends, economic dynamism, social solidarity, and an ethical response to progress in the life sciences are presented as issues that can no longer be effectively dealt with at a national level.

Not since the adoption of the Constitution of the United States of America in 1787 had a group of sovereign states agreed to accept a centralized government and a standardized system of laws that applied in all member states, guaranteeing the freedom of movement of people, goods, services, and capital. The EU maintained a common trade policy, agricultural and fisheries policies, and a regional development policy. Its member states adopted a common currency (the Euro) and developed a role in foreign policy, representing its members in the World Trade Organization, at summits of the world's biggest economies (G8), and at the United Nations. Twenty-one EU countries are members of NATO and have developed a role in justice and home affairs, including the abolition of passport control between many member states.

The EU was described as a hybrid of intergovernmentalism and supranationalism. In certain areas it depends on agreement between the member states, but it has supranational bodies, able to make decisions without the agreement of members. Important institutions and bodies of the EU include the European Commission, the European Parliament, the Council of the European Union, the European Council, European Court of Justice, and the European Central Bank. EU citizens elect the Parliament every five years.

After keeping the topics of its annual and sometimes twice-a-year meetings under wraps, the Bilderberg Group's almost total success in maintaining its discussions, membership rolls, and purposes private slowly came into view as the veil began to be drawn aside in 1975 by a handful of persistent probers who did not conform to conventional journalistic methods.

• Six •

THE SNOOPERS

The principal American publication to devote attention to the Bilderberg Group was the offspring of a Washington-based right-wing political action organization called the Liberty Lobby. According to its founder, Willis Carto, Bilderberg was a conspiracy of the global elite to plan a world government at the expense of national sovereignty and our constitutional rights. He wrote, "An extremely powerful lobby has developed among the community of international traders. Their loyalty is only to their money, wherever it may be and derived from whatever source. These capitalists are the greatest advocates of free trade and are implacable enemies of national sovereignty. They are far more dangerous to the nation than communists ever were."

Liberty Lobby described the New World Order as a "global plantation" in which nonproductive elites would live off the sweat of the world's producers. In Carto's view, "Today, the operating plan is a step-by-step progression to the final goal of ownership and control of all natural resources and every square inch of land and everything on it by a consortium of international supercapitalists."

Critics of Carto described him as antisemitic and the Liberty Lobby as a mechanism for Carto to expound hatred for Jews and his belief that they ran the world. Liberty Lobby's weekly newspaper, *The Spotlight*, claimed a national circulation of 200,000 and carried articles and editorials with a right-wing orientation based on suspicions of liberal big government and internationalism. *The Washington Post* has described *The Spotlight* as a "newspaper containing orthodox conservative political articles interspersed with anti-Zionist tracts and classified advertisements for Ku Klux Klan T-shirts, swastika-marked German coins, and cassette tapes of Nazi marching songs." When *The Spotlight* ceased publication in 2001 after Liberty Lobby was forced into bankruptcy as a result of a law suit, its employees started a similar newspaper called the *American Free Press*.

The Bilderberg reporter for both publications was James P. (Big Jim) Tucker, Jr. After working as an editor for the Associated Press, United Press International, and newspapers, he began writing about the Group for *The Spotlight* at the paper's outset. His efforts to infiltrate the 1999 Bilderberg meeting at the Hotel Caesar Park in Sintra, Portugal, were chronicled by British reporter Jon Ronson in his book *Them: Adventures with Extremists*. After Ronson, Tucker, and a cameraman waited at the hotel for several hours, Ronson expressed skepticism about whether anything would happen when a number of people began arriving in darkened limousines and buses. When Tucker said they were being tailed by a Bilderberg security team, Ronson was so shaken that he called the British Embassy asking for assistance.

In 2005, Tucker published *Jim Tucker's Bilderberg Diary*, a book chronicling his thirty-plus years of "exposing the Bilderberg Group." In the foreword, titled "Life in the Shadows with a Bilderberg Hound," American Free Press Midwest bureau chief Christopher Bollyn gave an account of accompanying Tucker to several Bilderberg meetings. "Over the course of those four years," he wrote, "I enjoyed being a part of the only American team of journalists that works to get inside Bilderberg and do what reporters are supposed to do: act as a watchdog for average Americans by disclosing truly important news."

Bollyn's first venture with Tucker began on Friday, May 31, 2000, with Bollyn's arrival on the day before the start of the Bilderberg meeting at the Chateau du Lac Hotel in Genval, near Brussels, Belgium. Told that he could have a room for only one night because the entire multimillion dollar resort would be taken over for the next four days "by a group of important people," he observed that conference rooms were being prepared. He also sensed that employees had been lectured to keep their mouths shut about the caliber of individuals who would be attending that coming weekend. The next morning, he looked out a window and saw a team of "special security agents walking around the front of the hotel."

As word spread among the locals that something unusual was going on at the Chateau du Lac, a crowd gathered along the road to the hotel. Bollyn found that he could see that Bilderberg security was becoming very uneasy with the scene in front of the hotel. The unexpected crowd had completely ruined their plans for the Bilderberg guests to slip into the hotel unnoticed. With dozens of people crowded around the front of the hotel there was very little Bilderberg security could do without drawing even more attention to the secretive group. "A few Bilderberg hounds, like Tony Gosling from England," Bollyn said, "were on hand and a young boy with a camera was even waiting by the front door trying to take photos of the rich and famous guests."

The next day, Bollyn arrived at the hotel early to find that two tents had been set up by the front door of the hotel. When a car arrived, it would drive into one tent so that the passengers could pass into the hotel without being seen. "I was busy running around trying to get photos of the individuals and groups as they walked near the lake," he recalled. "As long as I didn't get in anybody's way, there was very little Bilderberg security could do; the roadway was public property. The conference had just begun, but Bilderberg security decided that I had to go."

In front of the hotel, on public property, the security chief came up to Bollyn and stood directly in front of him. With burly arms crossed and a glowering frown, he said, "If you don't stop running behind people and taking pictures I'm going to jump all over you." Bollyn took his camera bag and went to a nearby restaurant and phoned Tucker to tell him what had happened. Tucker advised him to leave. On the street, two Belgian security thugs were watching. Bollyn called a taxi and waited for what seemed like ages. Finally, the taxi arrived and took him to the Brussels train station. He had to run across the tracks in front of the locomotive and jump on a train at the very last minute. He breathed a sigh of relief as the train pulled away from Brussels.

In June 2001, Bollyn was with Tucker for the Bilderberg Group's gathering at the Hotel Stenungsbaden near Gothenburg, Sweden. On the first day, while he was taking pictures from private property adjacent to the hotel with the permission of the owner, Swedish police seized him and drove him six miles into the wilderness and left him on the side of the road amidst farmers' fields. "I could see that with a large number of Swedish police helping Bilderberg, this was not going to be any easier than Belgium," he recalled. "On the other hand, thanks to our efforts, in Sweden there was more media coverage of the secretive group's meeting than in any other country I have seen."

At the hotel gate through which the Bilderberg cars had to pass, a group of witnesses from a variety of organizations were watching. Patriotic Swedes were aware that Bilderberg was meeting and were very interested to know who was attending and what was being discussed. Bollyn spent the next three days high up in a tree or on a breezy bridge overlooking the hotel waiting for a Bilderberger to come into view.

Compared to the event in Sweden, Bollyn noted, Bilderberg 2002, held at the Westfields Marriott hotel in Chantilly, Virginia, was a very lonely event. "It was completely different than in Europe," Bollyn wrote. "The Westfields Marriott is surrounded by trees, but Bilderberg 2002 didn't need much security because, apart from us, nobody seemed to care that the most powerful people in the Western world were meeting in secret for three days at the hotel. We met only one young man who had taken a bus from Phoenix, Arizona, to witness the Bilderberg meeting in Chantilly. As a long-time reader of *American Free Press* and *The*

Spotlight, he was very aware of the importance of what was happening in the Marriott hotel that weekend."

Describing encountering David Rockefeller as Bilderberg luminaries took a break from their meetings in Chantilly and gathered for dinner and drinks at the Great Hall of the Library of Congress's Thomas Jefferson Building in Washington, Tucker wrote that Rockefeller's smile froze and his eyeballs were spinning.

At 7 P.M., Tucker was stationed outside at the building's main entrance as long black limos began to roll up. As one luminary stepped out, Tucker smiled and said, "You are here for Bilderberg, too?"

"Yes," Rockefeller said with a smile.

At that point a guard said to Tucker, "You don't belong here."

Escorted out, Tucker protested, "I do, too, belong here because I am a taxpayer and they are conducting public business in secret."

"I have my orders, Mr. Tucker," said the guard in a gentle voice.

The following day, during public visiting hours, Tucker was "honored" with guards all day long. One would relieve the other. He observed Bilderberg people moving out of the room where they had been meeting and marching to another room at the opposite end of the building, down another long corridor. Tucker followed at the end of the line until the guard stopped him.

Another American Bilderberg snooper, syndicated radio talk show host, filmmaker, and conspiracy theorist Alex Jones, was born in Dallas, Texas, and attended the Austin Community College. He began his career in Austin with a live, call-in format cable-access television program. In 1996, he switched to KJFK and hosted The Final Edition. In 1997, he released his first documentary-style film, *America Destroyed by Design*. In early 2000, he was a Republican candidate for state representative in Texas House District 48, but withdrew before the March primary. On June 8, 2006, while he was on his way to cover a meeting of the Bilderberg group in Ottawa, Canada, he was stopped and detained at the Ottawa airport by Canadian authorities who confiscated his passport, camera equipment, and most of his belongings. He was later released. (He is not to be confused with the Alex Jones who is a Laurence M. Lombard Lecturer in the Press and Public Policy and Director of the Joan Shorenstein Center on the Press, Politics, and Public Policy of the Kennedy School of Government at Harvard University.)

The most persistent European tracker of Bilderbergers is Daniel Estulin. The author of *The True Story of the Bilderberg Group*, Estulin wrote of himself, "I'm a Russian ex-patriot who was kicked out of the Soviet Union in 1980. My father was a dissident who fought for freedom of speech who was jailed, tortured by the KGB. Suffered two political deaths. When these people got tired of us, they threw us out. We moved to Canada and twelve years ago I came to Spain. My grandfather was a colonel in the KGB and the [Soviet] counterintelligence in the 1950s, so I am privileged somewhat to get a lot of the information from secret service which are our best sources of information. Not only the KGB people but the MI6 people [British intelligence], the CIA because most of the people who work for the secret service as you probably know are patriots and they love their country and they're doing it for the good of the nation and they're the first ones absolutely terrified of the plans of the Bilderbergers."

Claiming to have been told about the Bilderberg Group in a Spanish restaurant in Toronto, Canada, in 1992, by a shadowy character named Vladimir, who may or may not have been a Soviet intelligence agent or working for some other spy organization, Estulin wrote that Vladimir's depiction of the Bilderberg Group as synonymous with "a One-World-Government takeover" turned his world upside down and changed his life forever.

Another Bilderberg watcher, Tony Gosling, was born in Gravesend, Kent, England, in 1962, and earned a humanities degree from Bradford University. After working for a few years in the family aviation business, he turned to radio journalism. After moving to Bristol, he took up investigative journalism and began tracking the Bilderbergers. He now describes himself as vice chair of the Bristol, England, branch of the National Union of Journalists.

For more than a quarter of a century, all these men to varying degree created careers out of accompanying the Bilderbergers to their meeting places, staking out the hotels, and employing whatever means and methods were at hand to identify the men who attended the conferences and to learn what transpired behind closed doors.

For a group that had been meeting since 1954 without drawing public attention, this sudden interest by journalists was itself partially responsible for heightened security and a reluctant decision by the Bilderberg Group to acknowledge its existence in the form of a press release. Given out prior to the conferences, they provided nothing to satisfy the hunger of the men whom Jim Tucker called "Bilderberg hounds" for details.

Typically, the press release concerning the June 8, 2006 meeting said only that "Bilderberg is a small, flexible, informal, and off-the-record international forum in which different viewpoints can be expressed and mutual understanding enhanced." It stated that all the participants "have agreed not to give interviews to the press" during or after the meeting, that there would not be a press conference, and that "it is an established rule that no attribution should be made" concerning what was discussed during the meeting. With the press release was an alphabetical list of the attendees, their nationalities, and their titles and affiliations with governments or other organizations. A third were from government and politics and the rest were from finance, industry, labor, education, and the media of communications.

"Imagine a private club," wrote Daniel Estulin, "where presidents, prime ministers, international bankers and generals rub shoulders, where gracious royal chaperones ensure everyone gets along, and where people running the wars, the markets, and Europe say what they never dare say in public. This is the Bilderberg Group, and it is the most secretive of any organization worldwide."

There have been occasions when a Bilderberger provided a peek behind the curtain of secrecy. Much of what became known about its beginnings came from books about its co-founders, Retinger and Bernhard. According to Alden Hatch in *H. R. H. Prince Bernhard of the Netherlands*, Bernhard had expressed concerns about the first meeting. "One thing that worries me beforehand," Bernhard said, "is suppose some key person does not show up and the discussions are a flop?"

One meeting Bernhard was particularly nervous about was the one at St. Simons Island, Georgia. United States senator J. William Fulbright and several other American congressmen were coming for the first time. One of Bernhard's American friends asked, "What are you going to do with the American politicians? You just can't shut up a United States congressman or senator. They aren't used to it."

"Bernhard didn't quite know himself," noted Hatch. "But before the meeting, he went to the American politicians, and in his most ingratiating way said, 'Gentlemen, my American friends are afraid to tell you this, but we have had this rule about five-minute speeches at our meetings. So would you be very kind and do me a favor, a personal favor, and stick to the rule, because I will be finished for the future if I let you get away with a long speech.'"

"They said they would be delighted; no problem at all . . ." recalled Bernhard. "And they never broke the rule at all. The only person I had trouble with was a European."

"The Bilderberg meetings were never dull," wrote Hatch. "Even though the group became 'like belonging to a fraternity,' sparks flew at nearly every one. . . . Hot issues were the Common Market and British and American attitudes toward it. There is always something to make the sparks fly," said Hatch, "and, like lightning, these electrical discharges clear the atmosphere.

"Any attempt to evaluate the effect of the Bilderberg Group was made nearly impossible by the very nature and object of the conferences. However, the intangible results are admittedly the greatest," noted Hatch.

An example was the case of the United States during Eisenhower's administration. When asked if he thought Eisenhower had been influenced by the Bilderberg discussions, Prince Bernhard said, "I don't know. Of course, I talked to Ike about it when I needed his help to give American officials the green light to come to the conferences. Although C. D. Jackson and Bedell Smith were in favor of it, there were a large number of people in the State Department who thought one should not go. They would not allow their people to come at first. Then after the first meeting they lifted the ban. Anybody could come. As to whether Ike paid any attention to the reports of our discussions, I could not say."

Eisenhower said, "I always had one of my people go to the Bilderberg Conferences [Dr. Gabriel Hauge]. I'm in favor of anything—any study of that kind which helps international understanding. The Bilderberg meetings enlightened me. I'd get viewpoints from other than official channels. Not that I always agreed with them; there were so many points of view that somebody had to be wrong; but it was still important to know them."

Under President Kennedy, the American government grew closer to Bilderberg because Kennedy had virtually staffed the State Department with what C. D. Jackson called "Bilderberg alumni." They included Secretary of State Dean Rusk, Undersecretary of State George W. Ball, advisors George McGhee, Walter Rostow, McGeorge Bundy, Arthur Dean, and Paul H. Nitze. George Ball said, "I think the most useful feature of the Bilderberg meetings is the opportunity for responsible people in industry, statecraft, or politics to have a frank discussion where they will not be publicly quoted and are able to give their personal views without their remarks being considered official."

"George Wildman Ball was born on December 19, 1909, in Des Moines, Iowa, and grew up in Des Moines and Evanston, Illinois, where the family moved in 1922 after his father received a promotion to the Standard Oil Company headquarters in Chicago. He attended

Northwestern and served as president of the university poetry society and first editor of a literary magazine. Graduated in 1930, he entered Northwestern Law School after briefly considering pursuing a doctorate in English ... and graduated in 1933 at the top of his class. When the law school dean nominated him for a position in the General Counsel's Office in the Farm Credit Administration, Ball headed off to Washington, DC., in May 1933. He moved to the Treasury Department in November 1933 and worked on international trade and tax legislation.

"Despite working on major New Deal policies, Ball felt his law training was too narrow and returned to the Midwest in 1935 to 'master the profession of law.' He joined a Chicago law firm as a tax attorney before moving to the prestigious firm of Sidley, McPherson, Austin & Harper in 1939.... During this time, he developed an interest in foreign affairs and began to attend Friday luncheons hosted by the Chicago Council on Foreign Affairs."

While serving in the General Counsel's Office of the Lend-Lease Administration, Ball met Jean Monnet. Accepting a position as a civilian member of the Air Force Evaluation Board to study the effects of tactical operations in Europe, he was appointed director of the Strategic Bombing Survey, which would appraise the whole strategic air offensive. In London in 1944, he appraised the effects of the air war against Germany, and in this capacity he worked with Monnet. Captivated by Monnet's vision of Europe as a unified political-economic entity that could be a bulwark of Western strength, Ball gave his support to the unification cause, becoming, in effect, its Washington representative after the war, as general counsel of the French Supply Council.

In this new assignment, Ball worked with Monnet to promote French recovery. When Ball returned to private law practice in July 1946, "Monnet retained his firm to represent the French government. Ball soon found himself conferring with Monnet's deputy on creation of the Organization for European Economic Cooperation (OEEC). He continued to work with Monnet on establishing a European economic plan throughout 1949, and it was this preliminary work that laid the foundation for the formation of the European Coal and Steel Community (ECSC). Despite his close relationship with Monnet, Ball was not involved in authorizing the final proposal, later known as the Schuman Plan, to establish a European common market for coal and steel under an independent authority.

"After ratification of the Treaty of Paris in August 1952, Ball was retained as the ECSC's adviser and later served as an adviser to the European Atomic Energy Community (Euratom) and the European Economic Community (EEC)." His interest in European affairs did not keep him from taking an interest in American politics. In 1952, he backed Adlai Stevenson in the presidential campaign, and in 1956 was director of public relations in Stevenson's second try at defeating Eisenhower. In 1960, as pressure mounted on Stevenson to endorse John F. Kennedy for the Democratic presidential nomination, he urged Stevenson not to.

After Kennedy won, Ball prepared a foreign policy analysis in Stevenson's name. Kennedy was so impressed that he appointed Ball undersecretary of state for economic affairs. In his new position, Ball worked on issues regarding trade and tariffs, economic affairs, the Congo, and European integration.

At a New York dinner honoring Jean Monnet on January 22, 1963, Ball read a letter from Kennedy that said, "For centuries, emperors, kings and dictators have sought to impose unity on Europe by force. For better or worse, they have failed. But under your inspiration, Europe has moved closer to unity in less than twenty years than it had done before in a thousand. You and your associates have built with the mortar of reason and the brick of economic and political interest. You are transforming Europe by the power of a constructive idea. Ever since the war the reconstruction and the knitting together of Europe have been objectives of United States policy, for we have recognized with you that in unity lies strength. And we have also recognized with you that a strong Europe would be good not only for Europeans but for the world. America and a united Europe, working in full and effective partnership can find solutions."

"It may be oversimplification," Bernhard said, "but I think that with a little bit of goodwill on both sides we will find practical solutions.

Within Europe itself, Bernhard would have liked to go even further than creating economic union.

Five years after the demise of the USSR and the end of European Communism, Jack Sheinkman, the chairman of the board of the Amalgamated Bank of Canada, provided a glimpse of the changed nature of the discussions. In an interview with reporter Trisha Katson, published in *The Spotlight*, on June 24, 1996, Sheinkman said that during the Group's meeting in Toronto the topics were "developments in Russia and China," the U.S. elections, and "establishing a common currency and market in Europe." Henry Kissinger chaired a panel on events in Israel and the impact on American foreign policy.

Noting that he had attended ten Bilderberg meetings and that he was a member of the Steering Committee, Sheinkman said that the annual Group conferences were "not just inconsequential gab fests." He proudly stated, "In some cases discussions do have an impact and become policy. The idea of a common [European] currency was discussed several years before it became policy. We had a discussion about the United States establishing formal relations with China before President Richard Nixon actually did it."

On the subject of the Bilderberg Group actually influencing governmental policies, Denis Healey opined that it was to be perfectly natural if an official decided to go home and implement a sensible policy he had heard discussed at a conference.

Where Healey, George Ball, and others saw nothing sinister in the Bilderberg Group, outsiders such as Tucker and Estulin suspected conspiracy. In an article titled "Plans to Destroy America Are Exposed" in the publication *American Almanac* dated August 11, 2002, journalist William Shannon wrote, "The Bilderbergers are searching for the age of post-nationalism when we won't have countries, but rather regions of the Earth surrounded by Universal values. That is to say, a global economy, one World government (selected rather than elected) and a universal religion. To assure themselves of reaching these objectives, the Bilderbergers focus on a greater technical approach and less awareness on behalf of the general public."

As part of this plan, the Bilderbergers are said to choose national leaders.

Seven

MAGGIE WOWS THE OLD BOY NETWORK

From its inception in 1954, the Bilderberg Group was a male-only organization. The only exception was Queen Beatrix of the Netherlands. Wives and mistresses were not allowed to attend. "Because women did not hold significant positions in governments in Europe and the United States in the first two decades," noted one journalist, "it wasn't surprising that the Group operated like an 'old boy network,' with the same names on the list of attendees year after year."

A dramatic departure from this policy occurred in 1975. As a founding father and member of the Steering Committee, Denis Healey proposed that an invitation be offered to a woman "back bench" Conservative (Tory) member of Parliament whom he described as "not worldly," but worthy of attention, if for no other reason than the fact that she was the leader of the Tories, and possibly a future prime minister.

"The daughter of a grocer, fifty-year-old Margaret Thatcher had graduated from Somerville College, Oxford, with a degree in chemistry, although she had always had an interest in politics and law. She ran for Parliament in 1950 but lost and continued to work as a research chemist. The following year she wed wealthy businessman Dennis Thatcher. The marriage enabled her to complete her studies for the bar and devote herself to politics. Although she again lost the election to Parliament in 1951, she had succeeded in winning the Conservative Finchely district seat in October 1959. Her first government posts were as joint parliamentary secretary of Pensions and National Insurance and as the secretary of Education and Science (1970–1974) under Prime Minister Edward Heath. After the Conservative Party lost two elections, she was supported by the very conservative right wing of the party. Criticizing Heath's economic policies, she had challenged him for the leadership of the Conservative Party, which she won in February 1975." This meant that if the Tories won the next election, she would become Britain's first woman prime minister.

Noting that she had accepted his invitation to the Bilderberg conference in the luxurious Golden Dolphin Hotel in Izmir, Turkey, in April 1975, Healey recalled, "She sat there for the first two days and didn't say a thing. Well, the invited guests must sing for their supper. They can't just sit there like a church mouse. They are there to speak. People started grumbling. A senator [Charles Mathias, Democrat of Maryland] came up to me on the Friday night and said, 'This lady you invited, she hasn't said a word. You really ought to say something to her.' "

Stating that, he had "a quiet word" with Thatcher at dinner. Healey observed, "She was embarrassed. Well, she obviously thought about it overnight, because the next day she stood up and launched into a three-minute Thatcher special. I can't remember the topic, but the room was stunned. As a result of that speech, David Rockefeller and Henry Kissinger and the other Americans fell in love with her. They brought her over to America, took her around in limousines, and introduced her to everyone."

Four years later, Thatcher became prime minister. Conspiracy theorists point to Thatcher's introduction to the Bilderbergers as proof that the Group has power to bestow its blessing on individuals and elevate them to positions of authority. Called the "Iron Lady" by the Soviet press and by detractors at home, Thatcher happily adopted the title. With the primary goal in her first term of enacting her ideas about how best to run the economy, denationalizing industry, and dismantling Socialism, she was saved from an increasing unpopularity of her economic policies by her personal handling of a war with Argentina over the British-held Falkland Islands in 1982.

Denis Healey attributed part of Britain's success in gaining global support for the war to the Bilderberg Group. He recalled that a "British government's request for international sanctions against Argentina for seizing the island colony fell on stony ground. But at a Bilderberg meeting in . . . Norway, [Foreign Secretary] David Owen stood up and gave the most fiery speech in favor of imposing them. The speech changed a lot of minds. I'm sure that foreign ministers went back to their prospective countries and told their leaders what David Owen had said. . . . Sanctions were imposed."

Riding a wave of victory-fed pride and patriotism to re-election in 1983, Thatcher was bolstered by a "short upturn in the economy that returned her to an unprecedented third term in 1987. Throughout all three terms she pursued economic policies that reduced the power of the unions, decreased public spending, increased personal tax cuts, increased privatization of public utilities, and deregulated industry. Recognized for having curbed runaway inflation and significantly reducing public spending and reducing the power of the British unions, in a program that became known as 'Thatcherism,'" she formed an alliance with President Ronald Reagan against the Soviet Union, strongly backed NATO, and endorsed deployment of U.S. Pershing and cruise missiles in Western Europe.

Her ideological and personal rapport with Reagan produced intense transatlantic cooperation between the United States and Britain, especially on issues related to the Soviet Union. In December 1984, when Mikhail Gorbachev visited London shortly before his elevation to general secretary of the Communist Party, Thatcher met with him. She came out of the discussions and said, "We can do business together."

Despite winning the general election in 1987, Thatcher was reported to have run afoul of the Bilderberg plan to create a European Union by refusing to allow Britain to join it. After being challenged for leadership of the Conservative Party, she resigned in November 1990. While she still held a parliamentary seat as a representative of Finchely, she did not run for reelection in 1992 and was made a baroness, giving her a seat in the House of Lords.

This sudden downfall has been attributed to the Bilderberg Group disaffection over her refusal to take Britain into the EU. Bilderberg critic Jim Tucker wrote that at the Group's meeting in La Toja, Spain, in 1989, Thatcher had been denounced for her provincialism and nationalism by insisting that Britain retain control over who enters the country instead of accepting passports of the superstate and not surrendering sovereignty to the European superstate. Tucker claimed that the weekend of May 11–14, 1989, was spent "plotting" her "political assassination."

Whether or not the Bilderberg Group was responsible for Thatcher's rise to power and for ringing down the curtain on her political career can never be verified.

Eight

BILDERBERG AND THE EVIL EMPIRE

During her years as prime minister, Margaret Thatcher had forged a political and personal friendship with a president of the United States who entered the White House with a simple formula for dealing with the fifty-year Cold War with the Soviet Union: "We win, they lose."

In a speech during the 1980 presidential campaign, Republican candidate Ronald Reagan declared, "We are faced with the most evil enemy mankind has known in his long climb from the swamp to the stars." Warning of the threat to freedom from the Soviet Union and the peril of the spread of Communism around the world, including the Western Hemisphere, he was ridiculed by opponents who said his ideas were naive. He agreed that in a world of complex questions, there were no easy answers. But, he said, "There are simple answers."

Democratic Party presidential advisor Clark Clifford said Reagan was "an amiable dunce." To Robert Wright of the magazine *New Republic* he was "virtually brain dead." In *Harper's Magazine*, Nicholas von Hoffman called him an "unlettered, self-assured bumpkin." Many Democrats thought he was "a reckless cowboy" and "simple-minded ideologue."

In a Cold War world of missiles with nuclear warheads stockpiled in the thousands by hostile superpowers on both sides of the Iron Curtain, his critics exclaimed that such talk was at the very least dangerous, if not insane. His ideas were so foolishly outdated that they represented a romantic view of a world that was found only in movies in which Ronald Reagan had once made a living as an actor.

Born on February 6, 1917, in Tampico, Illinois, he grew up in nearby Dixon, spent summers as a lifeguard and saved scores of people from drowning, worked his way through Eureka College, became a radio announcer in Iowa, made fifty-three movies, and was twice elected governor of California. Calling himself "the Gipper," taken from the name of the character George Gipp, that he had played in the film about the 1930s University of Notre Dame football coach Knute Rockne. He went around the country offering "simple" solutions to the nation's problems in the form of lower taxes, smaller federal government, and an alternative to the old policy of containment of Communism through a strengthened military with a mission to not only stop the spread of Communism, but also vanquish it.

His Democratic opponent in 1980 was Jimmy Carter. As governor of Georgia, he was said to have been viewed by the Bilderbergers as a rising political star who appeared to share the Group's globalist views. During his presidency, he had advisors who were frequent Bilderberg attendees.

Dispirited by rampant inflation and disheartened by Carter's inability to liberate Americans from the humiliation of being held hostage for more than a year in Iran, an overwhelming majority of American voters elected Reagan. Although he scored a stunning electoral victory over Carter and helped to gain a Republican majority in the U.S. Senate, Democrats who dominated the House not only strongly opposed his domestic agenda of smaller federal government and large tax cuts but also clung to Harry S. Truman's initiated policy of "containment" of Communism, Dwight D. Eisenhower's search for "peaceful coexistence," Richard Nixon's policy of "detente," and Carter's policy of negotiating with the Soviet Union from a weak position.

In a rising tide of pessimism and a gloomy sense that America was an impotent country and ready to accept a continuing stalemate with the Soviet Union and moral equivalency between Communism and democracy, Reagan offered a sunny optimism and confidence that his opponents predicted would result in abject failure at home and across the world. Nothing proved this point, exclaimed Democrats, liberal newspaper columnists, and other Washington and New York pundits, more than a speech Reagan delivered in London, England, to the House of Commons on June 8, 1982. With numerous Bilderbergers present, he answered the critics and prophets of gloom by declaring, "We're approaching the end of a bloody century plagued by a terrible political invention—totalitarianism. Optimism comes less easily today, not because democracy is less vigorous, but because democracy's enemies have refined their instruments of repression. Yet optimism is in order because day by day democracy is proving itself to be a not at all fragile flower."

If history teaches anything, he said, it is that self-delusion in the face of unpleasant facts is folly. "We see around us today," he asserted, "the marks of our terrible dilemma, predictions of doomsday, anti-nuclear demonstrations, an arms race in which the West must, for its own protection, be an unwilling participant. At the same time we see totalitarian forces in the world who seek subversion and conflict around the globe to further their barbarous assault on the human spirit."

He asked, "What, then, is our course? Must civilization perish in a hail of fiery atoms? Must freedom wither in a quiet, deadening accommodation with totalitarian evil?" The mission of the United States, Great Britain, and the West was "to preserve freedom as well as peace." Stating that "we live now at a turning point," he saw "a great revolutionary crisis, a crisis where the demands of the economic order are conflicting directly with those of the political order. But the crisis is happening not in the free, non-Marxist West but in the home of Marxism-Leninism, the Soviet Union. It is the Soviet Union that runs against the tide of history by denying human freedom and human dignity to its citizens."

Describing the USSR as a "failure" of "overcentralized" government "with little or no incentives," he noted that year after year "the Soviet system pours its best resources into the making of instruments of destruction. The constant shrinkage of economic growth combined with the growth of military production is putting a heavy strain on the Soviet people. What we see here is a political structure that no longer corresponds to its economic base, a society where productive forces are hampered by political ones."

It is "the democratic countries that are prosperous and responsive to the needs of their people," Reagan said. "And one of the simple but overwhelming facts of our time is this: of all the millions of refugees we've seen in the modern world, their flight is always away from, not toward, the Communist world."

While Reagan was obviously an internationalist, he was also clearly a nationalist and differed from the Bilderberg view of a world in which boundaries would disappear. Although he never attended a Bilderberg meeting, ten members of the team that planned the transition between Reagan and Carter were Bilderbergers, including his designees for secretary of state (James Baker) and secretary of the treasury (George Shultz). So was the vice president-elect, George Herbert Walker Bush.

Because the Bilderberg Group was formed to foster European unity and strengthen ties between Europe and the United States in the face of a Communist threat, the sudden end of the Cold War during the Reagan years and the collapse of the Soviet Union would seem to have left the Group purposeless. This was not the case. "The Cold War has now ended," said a Bilderberg Group press release. "But in practically all aspects there are more, not fewer problems—from trade to jobs, from monetary policy to investment, from ecological problems to the task of promoting international security. It is hard to think of any major issue in Europe and North America whose unilateral solution would not have repercussions for the other. Thus the concept of a European-American forum has not been overtaken."

In defeating Communism and causing the downfall of the Soviet Union, Reagan had also removed the obstacle that had held back the Bilderberg plan not only for a unified Europe but for what conspiracy seekers discern as its grander scheme to create a New World Order. When Joseph Retinger met with Bernhard in 1954 to propose a meeting on the subject of European unification, the political leaders, international bankers, and prominent figures who settled comfortably into the Bilderberg Hotel had on their agenda a Europe that was struggling to complete a recovery from the most destructive and bloody conflict in history. They also had a fractured continent that since 1945 had come to be known in the shorthand of the Cold War as "the Free World."

On January 20, 1953, the nature of the divide had been defined by America's new president. In his inaugural address, Dwight D. Eisenhower had said, "In Europe, we ask that enlightened and inspired leaders of the Western nations strive with renewed vigor to make the unity of their peoples a reality."

Half a century after Eisenhower's appeal, and two decades after the collapse of the Soviet Union, the announcement came that the Bilderbergers gathering for the fifty-fourth meeting, to be held in Ottawa, Canada, would have on the agenda European-American relations, energy, Russia, Iran, terrorism, and immigration.

According to observers of the Bilderberg Group, the original purpose presented by Retinger to create a European-American alliance against the threat to Western capitalism by Soviet communism was transformed after the collapse of the USSR by international bankers, "globalists," and idealists into a grand scheme to slowly establish a worldwide government.

In the view of one unofficial historian of the Bilderberg Group, the intention of the meetings of these bankers, politicians, and intellectuals was the creation of an "aristocracy of purpose" between Europe and the United States. They discussed how to achieve agreement on questions of policy, economics, and strategy in "jointly ruling the world."

The purpose of the post–Cold War meetings was to review and discuss the current world situation, anticipate future events so as to shape or control them, and agree on which policies must be carried out by government to achieve these goals. Conservative author Phyllis Schlafly wrote in *A Choice Not an Echo* that the Group became "a little clique of powerful men who meet secretly and plan events that appear to 'just happen.' "

Meeting without the public being aware of their conferences, the Group allegedly devised plans to draw the world gradually into a global system of government and finance in which national sovereignty would be erased and replaced by "globalization," in which banks and multinational corporations ruled.

Until a world government could be established, these goals were to be fostered by political leaders chosen by the Bilderberg Group. Legislative leaders would be invited to Group meetings to be educated about policies to promote globalism, such as regional free trade treaties, as well as educational programs to advance globalism, in the expectation that they would return to their capitals to draft legislation to achieve them.

Bilderberg critic and journalist Daniel Allen Rivera wrote that a program called "Goals 2000," developed during the presidency of George W. Bush to revamp America's public school system, had been born at the April 1970 meeting in Bad Ragaz, Switzerland. The goal of the new educational philosophy was said to be the "subordination of national ambitions to the idea of the international community" because existing schools were "too nationalistic." The goal was to teach students to consider themselves "world citizens." Rivera also noted that prior to the 1971 meeting in Woodstock, Virginia, Bernhard said that the subject of the meeting was a "change in the world role of the United States."

It is also contended that at the 1978 meeting, the Group discussed replacing the U.S. dollar with an international bank note called the "bancor" that would be universally acceptable as a medium of exchange. The bancor would be backed by a world gold reserve deposited in a neutral country.

At their 1990 meeting at Glen Cove, Long Island, in New York, the Bilderbergers supposedly decided that U.S. taxes had to be raised to pay more toward the debts owed to international bankers. Although George H. W. Bush had pledged during his presidential campaign that he would not impose new taxes, he found himself coming under pressure from Bilderbergers to sign one of the biggest tax increases in history.

During the 1991 Bilderberg meeting at the Black Forest Resort in Baden-Baden, Germany, the group supposedly discussed plans for a common European currency and European central banking. David Rockefeller is said to have argued during the meeting that "supranational sovereignty of an intellectual elite and world bankers" was "preferable" to the nationalism that had prevailed for centuries.

When the Group assembled in Évian-les-Bains, France, on May 21, 1992, the nature of the Europe that existed when the Group formed in 1954 had been changed dramatically. In a rapid and almost bewildering upheaval that began in November 1989 with the opening of the Berlin Wall, the Soviet empire that Ronald Reagan had vowed to destroy had unraveled like a worn-out wool sweater. In August of 1991, in a last-ditch effort to save the Soviet Union, already floundering under the impact of the political movements that had emerged since the implementation of Mikhail Gorbachev's glasnost, a group of hard-line Communists organized a coup, kidnapped Gorbachev, and announced on state television that Gorbachev was very ill and would no longer be able to govern. As massive protests were staged in Moscow, Leningrad, and other major cities of the Soviet Union, the coup organizers tried to bring in the military to quell the protestors, but the soldiers rebelled. After three days of protests, the coup organizers surrendered. The Soviet Union collapsed, replaced by a Commonwealth of Republics composed of fifteen independent countries. With the Soviet empire that Reagan labeled "evil" gone, leaving the United States as the world's only superpower, the Bilderberg goal of an EU as a stepping-stone on the way toward a capitalist world government controlled by an elite appeared attainable.

The Cold War was barely over in 1992, wrote Jim Tucker, when the "Bilderberg boys" planned to exploit the rich natural resources, cheap land, property, and labor in the former Soviet Union. For the first time, he noted, there was "a major presence" of men from the former USSR, requiring the meeting to take over two hotels at the resort, the Royal and Ermitage, and "the tightest security of any meeting so far."

Also on the minds of the Bilderbergers at Évian was the presidential election in the United States. Challenging George H. W. Bush, deemed by political pollsters to be in trouble for having abandoned his 1988 campaign pledge of "no new taxes," was the young man who, as the governor of Arkansas had made a powerful impression when he attended in 1991.

• Nine •

Bubba and the Bilderbergs

Among the Americans at the Bilderberg meeting in Baden-Baden, Germany, in 1991, were Group regulars David Rockefeller, Henry Kissinger, Secretary of the Treasury Nicholas F. Brady, Rhode Island senator John Chaffee, former San Francisco mayor and future U.S. senator Dianne Feinstein, Katharine Graham of *The Washington Post*, Louisiana senator J. Bennett Johnston, ambassador to the Soviet Union Jack F. Matlock, Jr., William B. Quand of the Brookings Institute, Citicorp CEO John S. Reed, Virginia governor Douglas Wilder, United Steel Workers president Lynn R. Williams, and Vernon Eulion Jordan, a Washington lawyer and wheeler-dealer described in a *Washington Post* profile as "a presidential adviser without title or salary," "a lawyer who rarely steps into a courtroom, who seldom writes a brief or motion," and "a lobbyist who does not lobby, at least not in the official sense of the term."

A civil rights leader who some said had forsaken his early ideals in a successful quest for a place at the seat of national power. Vernon Eulion Jordan, Jr., was a black man who had achieved an unprecedented, unparalleled stature as a Washington power broker, reaching the pinnacle of one of the most obstinately white workplaces in the nation.

The grandson of a sharecropper, Jordan was a multimillionaire who resided in a Washington, DC, mansion and hobnobbed with cabinet members, CEOs of the world's largest corporations, and television anchors. Following a decade of running the National Urban League, he had joined one of Washington's most powerful law firms and sat on the boards of eleven major companies. It was that he had spurned an opportunity to become the first black Attorney General of the United States because he said he would rather not open his accounts to public view.

Regardless of his race, Jordan was exactly the kind of person always welcomed to Bilderberg ranks. When Jordan brought a guest to the 1991 conference, the newcomer at first glance seemed to possess none of the worldly traits expected of the conferees. Born William Jefferson Blythe III on August 19, 1946, in Hope, Arkansas, he lost his father in an auto accident and when his mother remarried he took the name of his stepfather, Roger Clinton of Hot Springs, Arkansas. A graduate of Georgetown University, Bill Clinton was awarded a Rhodes Scholarship to Oxford and then earned a law degree from Yale (1973). After his graduation, he returned to Arkansas and taught law at the University of Arkansas before entering politics. His 1974 campaign for Congress ended in defeat, but two years later he was elected Arkansas attorney general.

In 1975, he had married Hillary Rodham, whom he had met while a law student at Yale. Elected governor of Arkansas in 1978, he lost a bid for reelection in 1980, but he regained the governorship two years later and served until 1993. In 1989, the executive director of the Democratic Leadership Council (DLC), Al From, had made a visit to Little Rock, Arkansas, and asked Clinton to become chairman of the DLC. Founded in 1984 by a group of moderate Southern politicians, the DLC declared that its goal was to move the Democratic Party toward the center of the political spectrum. By becoming its president, Clinton assured himself of a national stage from which to advance not only the aims of the DLC but his lifelong goal of running for president of the United States.

Although there is no public record of what Clinton said when he was called upon to give the required three-minute address to the Bilderbergers in 1991, the widely held belief of Bilderberg observers is that his appearance equaled or surpassed the acclaim given to Margaret Thatcher and persuaded the Bilderbergers to pave the way for Clinton to run against President George H. W. Bush in the 1992 election. Believers that the Bilderberg Group's goal is to control the world claim that although H. W. Bush had pledged Americans that there would be no new taxes while he was president, the Group pressured him to break the promise in order to finance loan repayments to international banks. But when it soon became clear that the Bush tax increase doomed Bush's chances for re-election, the Group exerted its influence to secure the Democratic nomination for Clinton.

Those who believe the Bilderberg Group is working to create a New World Order cite as evidence of its power that it was able to elevate to the presidency the obscure governor of a small southern state with a drawl that caused him to come across as a "good old boy" and a "bubba," rather than a sophisticated Rhodes Scholar, Yale Law graduate, and shrewd political thinker.

When Clinton took office on January 20, 1993, the Congress had before it a treaty that Bilderberg critics viewed as advancing the Group plan of globalization. Known as the North American Free Trade Agreement (NAFTA), it was between the United States, Mexico, and Canada and signed in December 1992 by President George H. W. Bush (allegedly at the urging of the Bilderberg Group), Canadian prime minister Brian Mulroney, and Mexican president Carlos Salinas de Gortari. The treaty eliminated trade barriers. Despite considerable opposition in all three countries, President Bill Clinton made its ratification a major legislative priority in 1993. After intense political debate, the House of Representatives passed it on November 17, 1993, and the Senate followed suit on the last day of its 1993 session (November 20, 1993).

Implementation began on January 1, 1994. The agreement would remove most barriers to trade and investment among the United States, Canada, and Mexico. All nontariff barriers to agricultural trade between the United States and Mexico were eliminated. In addition, many tariffs were removed immediately, with others being phased out over periods of five to fifteen years. This allowed for an orderly adjustment to free trade with Mexico, with full implementation beginning January 1, 2008.

Few international agreements entered into by American presidents proved to be more controversial. While U.S. labor unions claimed that NAFTA would result in the loss of jobs by encouraging American industries to shift operations from the United States to countries with lower wage scales, others warned of a flood of illegal immigrants from Mexico. Bilderberg watchers saw the treaty as a giant step toward globalization that was to be realized under the provisions of an earlier, broader General Agreement on Tariffs and Trade (GATT) and the Asia-Pacific Economic Community (APEC).

An Australian publication, *The Age*, found GATT, NAFTA and APEC part of a push for a one-world economic system run by the free trade imperatives of multinational consortiums and international financiers. "With the consent of representatives of 116 nations, including the enthusiastic endorsement of the Australian Government," said the article, "the GATT aims to put the nail in the coffin of national independence and self-reliance. In the approving words of U.S. insider Strobe Talbott, the GATT will determine "trade, finance and development for a united world."

In an article in *Time* magazine entitled "The Birth of the Global Nation," Talbott had said, "I'll bet that within the next 100 years, nationhood as we know it will be obsolete; all states will recognize a single global authority."

"Talbott echoes the sentiments of capitalist globalist apologists like Australian foreign minister Gareth Evans," said *The Age*. As he sees it,

"All countries are basically social arrangements. No matter how permanent and even sacred they may seem at any one time, in fact they are all artificial and temporary."

Clinton's trade representative, Mickey Kantor, briefing the press at the conclusion of a GATT meeting in Brussels, Belgium, had said that how NAFTA and the Asia-Pacific Economic Community will "fit in" with GATT is still "to be decided." He added, "You can't achieve everything in your first agreement."

Addressing an APEC meeting in Seattle, Washington, Clinton had said, "The Asia-Pacific region should be a united one, not divided." Kim Young Sam, president of South Korea, agreed, stating that the APEC countries should "gradually develop into an Asia-Pacific Economic Community." Critics of NAFTA, GATT, and APEC called them the most far-reaching free trade agreements in history and said they effectively destroyed the national economies, subjecting them to imperatives of world trade and control of plutocratic elites.

More than a decade after NAFTA went into effect, it remained a matter of contention. In the pro-globalization *Washington Post* on February 8, 2006, Harold Meyerson observed, "The public is skeptical, rightly, about the benefits of globalization, but the process of harnessing it, of writing enforceable rules that would benefit not just investors but most of our citizens, is hard to even conceive. And so globalization is experienced by many Americans as a loss of control. . . . With the number of immigrants illegally in the United States estimated at 11 million," Meyerson noted, "the tensions between Americans and Mexicans, chiefly the working-class Americans and working-class Mexicans, are rising." He pointed out that "over 40 percent of the Mexicans who had come, legally and illegally, to the United States had done so in the past 15 years. The boom in undocumenteds was even more concentrated. There were just 2.5 million undocumented immigrants in the United States in 1995. Eight million had arrived since then."

"It's not because we've let down our guard at the border; to the contrary, the border is more militarized now than it's ever been," wrote Meyerson. "The answer is actually simpler than that. In large part, it's NAFTA. The North American Free Trade Agreement was sold, of course, as a boon to the citizens of the United States, Canada and Mexico—guaranteed both to raise incomes and lower prices, however improbably, throughout the continent. Bipartisan elites promised that it would stanch the flow of illegal immigrants, too."

Citing Economist Jeff Faux in a report of the effects of NAFTA titled "The Global Class War," Meyerson noted that "Mexico had been home to a poor agrarian sector for generations, which the Mexican government helped sustain through price supports on corn and beans, but NAFTA had put those farmers in direct competition with incomparably more efficient U.S. agribusinesses. It proved to be no contest: From 1993 through 2002, at least two million Mexican farmers were driven off their land. The experience of Mexican industrial workers under NAFTA had not been a whole lot better. In the pre-NAFTA days of 1975, Mexican wages came to 23 percent of U.S. wages. In 1993–1994, just before NAFTA, they amounted to 15 percent; and by 2002 they had sunk to 12 percent." A free trade agreement that was said to have been inspired by the Bilderberg Group, negotiated by George H. W. Bush, and pushed through Congress by Bill Clinton, NAFTA was not only embraced by President George W. Bush but held up as evidence that all of the regional and global impediments to trade should be removed. To that end, he presented a free trade agreement with Colombia to a Democrat-controlled Congress in the election year of 2008. When it was put on a legislative back burner by Speaker of the House Nancy Pelosi, the result was an eruption of public resentment against globalization in general and NAFTA in particular. On April 9, 2008, *The Washington Post* reported, "The North American Free Trade Agreement is once again a prime scapegoat for the nation's growing economic troubles, drawing blame for sending jobs overseas and flattening wages for U.S. workers. That sentiment has intensified as the economy has deteriorated, a fall punctuated last week by the steepest job decline in five years."

At the epicenter of the anti-free trade, anti-NAFTA eruption were Senators Hillary Clinton and Barack Obama as they campaigned ahead of the Pennsylvania Democratic primary on April 22, 2008. Facing voters in a state that had lost more than 200,000 manufacturing jobs since 2001, Obama had promised to stand against trade deals that cost U.S. jobs, while saying Clinton had supported NAFTA in the past.

Stating that she had always opposed the deal, even as her husband signed it as president, Clinton said, "I don't think NAFTA has been good for America."

After doing some fact-checking, *The Washington Post* discovered that many leading economists did not agree with Clinton and Obama. "It is true that the United States has lost about 4 million manufacturing jobs since 1994, the year NAFTA went into effect and eliminated most hurdles to trade and investment between the United States, Mexico and Canada," reporter Meyerson said. "Not only are items such as clothing, toys and televisions increasingly made abroad, but so are more complex goods including sophisticated magnets that help steer military smart bombs and radio frequency identification chips embedded in new U.S. passports. But many economists blame the march of technology and the increasingly dominant manufacturing role of China, not NAFTA, for that shift."

The economists said that "NAFTA had been a net plus for the U.S. economy. Even as the number of factory jobs dropped, manufacturing output in the United States was up 58 percent between 1993 and 2006, as U.S. plants produced more goods with fewer workers. Exports were at a record high, and trade among the three NAFTA partners had tripled since 1994. Meanwhile, overall employment in the United States had grown 24 percent and average unemployment is down since NAFTA went into effect. Some cities along the border with Mexico had grown, and farm exports had gone up.

"The escalating debate over the future of free-trade agreements promises to be a stark fault line in the campaign, Meyerson wrote, noting that Arizona senator John McCain, the presumptive Republican nominee for president, was an unabashed supporter of free trade.

"Even with all their objections to these trade deals," Meyerson recorded, "Obama and Clinton were careful about where and when they attacked NAFTA. While campaigning in Pennsylvania and earlier in Ohio, both places where trade was blamed for job losses, they pledged to withdraw from the NAFTA treaty if it were not renegotiated to toughen labor and environmental standards. But the candidates were mostly silent on the deal in Texas, where economists said it had increased exports, not only to Mexico, but also to Canada, Europe, Latin American and Asia. Some top congressional Democrats have said that rather than renegotiate NAFTA, which analysts called a difficult proposition likely to produce strong demands from the Canadians and Mexicans, who have their own problems with the treaty—the candidates should focus on easing the transition of workers into the new economy."

In reviewing the history of NAFTA, analysts pointed out that it was all but impossible to separate the impact of NAFTA from other economic changes that unfolded before and since it was implemented, including other free trade deals, increased competition from manufacturers from Eastern Europe to India, and, most significantly, China's rise.

Lawrence H. Summers, a Harvard University professor who served as treasury secretary under President Clinton, claimed he was proud to have supported NAFTA. NAFTA, he said, had bolstered the economy and improved national security, while easing U.S. problems with illegal immigration.

"The forces that are driving job dislocations are not primarily trade related," Summers said. "They are technological improvements, increases in the productive capacity of developing nations and technology that enables greater global integration."

"NAFTA had gone into effect with promises that it would be an economic boon to North America. By eliminating tariffs among the United States, Mexico, and Canada and liberalizing foreign investment in Mexico, proponents had said, the continent would end up with lower prices and higher wages. As living standards rose, the economic incentives fueling illegal immigration would evaporate, boosters said, and exports fostered by the world's largest free-trade zone would add 200,000 U.S. jobs. Proponents predicted that the pact would help convert small trade deficits with Mexico and Canada into surpluses."

Critics of NAFTA argued that "fourteen years later, illegal immigration across the southern border had skyrocketed. Meanwhile, average wages stagnated in the United States and Mexico, and the U.S. trade deficits with Canada and Mexico ballooned. Hundreds of U.S. textile mills closed as Mexican-made apparel was allowed into the country duty free. Many of those operations had since come under strong pressure from competition in China. Also hurt were workers at manufacturing concerns in the industrial Midwest and in other areas. Many saw well-paying jobs move out and wages squeezed. Defense of NAFTA came from Philippe Legrain. Author of *Immigrants: Your Country Needs Them*, he wrote, "Senator Hillary Rodham Clinton often likes to take credit for her husband's achievements as president. But then there's NAFTA. Clinton may have been present at the creation of the North American Free Trade Agreement in 1994, but she wants everybody to know that it's not her baby. She now proposes to 'fix' the agreement to make trade 'work for working families.'"

To the charge that "NAFTA has transformed the U.S. economy," Legrain replied, "Hardly. Critics rightly point out that NAFTA's economic benefits were oversold, but they're wrong to heap the blame for all America's woes on it." NAFTA, he said, which expanded the existing Canadian-U.S. free-trade area to Mexico, has had only a minimal effect on the U.S. economy. True, he said, exports to Mexico had more than

tripled since 1993—but at $161 billion, they still accounted for only
1.1 percent of the economy.

Had NAFTA put countless Americans out of work?

"Not really," wrote Legrain, Obama claimed that NAFTA has destroyed a million American jobs. Even if he was correct, total employment still rose by 27 million jobs between 1993 and 2007, to 137.6
million. At worst, then, he claimed, NAFTA has cost only a tiny minority of American workers their jobs.

Campaigning in Erie, Pennsylvania, in the spring of 2008 in support of his wife Hillary's bid for the Democratic presidential nomination, Clinton returned fire at a heckler who began shouting about
Clinton's attendance at the 1991 Bilderberg conference and implying
that the discussions there had led to NAFTA and American job losses.
As the audience booed the heckler, Clinton replied, "All right, here's the
answer. I happened to be in Europe then on my way to Russia. I was invited to go to Bilderberg by Vernon Jordan, a friend of mine and a genu-
ine hero of the civil rights movement. And to the best of my knowledge
NAFTA was not discussed by anybody in my presence. Number two,
I tried to get labor and environmental standards in the agreement but
I couldn't because it was all negotiated when I got there [to the White
House]. Number three, when I was president, we enforced our trade
laws five times as much as the Bush administration did."

As for attending the Bilderberg conference, Clinton said, "I had a
very good time talking to those Europeans about European affairs and
what was going to happen to Russia, but I was not somehow polluted
by it into sacrificing America's economic interests. America did a lot
better when I was president than they did in this decade. And that's
the truth."

• Ten •

THE FIRST POST-NATIONAL WAR

As the Bilderbergers gathered on June 7, 1991, at the Badischer Hof hotel in Baden-Baden, Germany, the talk was of a historic decision by President George H. W. Bush in January to use American military power to crush an invasion of Kuwait by Iraq that had been launched in the previous summer by Iraqi dictator Saddam Hussein for the purpose of seizing and controlling its oil fields. What pleased the Bilderbergers as much as Bush's unprecedented military response, the brevity of the fighting, and the destruction of Iraq's army, had been Bush's decision to seek approval of the action to repel the Iraqis from the United Nations Security Council.

Noting that for the first time since the Korean War in 1950 American troops had been sent to war as a United Nations force, several speakers surmised that if Americans could be persuaded to allow their armed forces to become an international force, the end of "parochial nationalism" was an attainable goal. Said one participant, "The Persian Gulf venture has advanced the cause for years."

Referring to the low casualty rate among U.S. forces, and pointing out how avidly the American public had watched television coverage of the war, another speaker said that they "enjoyed it like an international sporting match."

Henry Kissinger was reported to have told a forum on the subject of the Bilderberg goal of ultimately fashioning a global army at the disposal of the United Nations. "A UN army must be able to act immediately, anywhere in the world, without the delays involved in each country making its own decision whether to participate, based on parochial considerations." It was also said that Bush seeking UN approval of the war before he followed the U.S. Constitution's requirement to obtain Congressional permission was a significant step in "leading Americans away from nationalism."

Among the effects of the demise of the Soviet Union and the end of its control of the countries of Eastern Europe was the dissolution of Yugoslavia into ethnic, religious, and historic areas that demanded independence. In February 1998, the Serbian president, Slobodan Milosevic, sent troops into one of these regions (Kosovo) to take back land-controlled areas by rebels. Eighty people were killed. The violence against civilians sparked rioting that escalated into a war and the first intervention by NATO in a conflict between a sovereign nation and its citizens. NATO justified military action by citing a responsibility to prevent crimes against humanity. After months of unsuccessful attempts at restoring peace, it resorted to military action in the form of bombing raids that began on March 24, 1999.

Two months later, the forty-seventh Bilderberg conference was held at the Caesar Park Hotel Penha Longa, Sintra, Portugal. From June 3 to 6, the 111 representatives of 24 countries gathered as Milosevic prepared to surrender to NATO. Although the Group followed its policy of keeping details of its meetings secret, a copy of a report containing a summary of the proceedings made its way into the hands of outsiders and provided details of what had transpired on the subject of Kosovo.

Some participants declared the Kosovo war a success. Some called it the first "post–nationalist war" and said that it solidified the EU and reconfigured foreign policy based on universal values rather than national interests. Most of the speakers worried that the conflict had left the Balkans devastated and strained relations with Russia and China.

"The fundamental fact about Kosovo," said the first of four panelists on the subject, "is that we won and Milosevic lost. The victory was far from ideal, however. We went in the right direction for the right reason but with the wrong means. And it raises a troubling question: are there causes that are worth killing for but not worth dying for? The war marks our entry into a new world in which national sovereignty is not the ultimate ratio of political life. It is highly significant that the war broke out on the same day in March that the House of Lords passed its verdict on General Pinochet. The war also gave a new meaning to the term Europe: much more so than the Euro which was launched three months before the conflict was started. Part of what it means to be a European is to refuse to accept ethnic cleansing."

In a summary of the Kosovo discussion that omitted the names of the speakers, the first panelist was recorded as stating that war raised questions about both the United States and Russia. "What price was the United States willing to pay to remain the world's only hyper-power? The answer given by Kosovo was far from clear, with America willing to deploy its 'soft power' but much more reluctant about its 'hard power.' . . . As for Russia, it was coming out of an age of interventionist imperialism at precisely the time when the rest of the world is entering a new age of interest in humanitarian causes," while "Russia was being told to exercise restraint at exactly the same time that the rest of the world is embracing intervention."

The second panelist declared, "Kosovo is a long-standing legacy of the Ottoman and Habsburg Empires and their failure to install a proper political system in the region. It will thus last for many years to come."

"The war was marred by three serious problems. NATO used force as a substitute for diplomacy rather than a support for it. It failed to understand the real nature of the conflict: This was not a matter of quick fixes but one of long-term management and containment. And it used force in a way that minimized danger to itself but maximized danger to the people it was trying to protect."

"Kosovo is now a wasteland," said the panelist, "a humanitarian disaster comparable with Cambodia; the region around it has been profoundly destabilized, and Serbia is in danger of imploding. We cannot solve the Balkan problem without the help of Serbia, which overshadows the region in much the same way that Germany overshadows Europe. But Serbia's leaders have been indicted as war criminals, and the country is likely to be racked with social problems, fueled by despair. We may be entering the twenty-first century in calendar terms. But in political terms we are much closer to the nineteenth."

The third panelist stated, "The war in Kosovo stems from the fact that the 'solution' to the Bosnia problem was nothing of the sort. It failed to address the security concerns of the major players and left two of the three ethnic groups that make up the new country wishing they were somewhere else. If we remove troops from Bosnia, the conflict will reignite immediately. In Kosovo, the West used NATO in a way that the rest of the world thought was illegitimate: it intervened in an area that was not its prime responsibility; and it did not bother to get the endorsement of the United Nations."

The discussion's moderator said, "It was a mistake to let the war in Kosovo happen (though we had no choice but to win once war had been declared). We have devastated the region that we were trying to save purely in order to avoid suffering casualties ourselves. We allowed the agenda to be set by domestic pressure groups, thus making it difficult to end the war. And we established a principle that the rest of the world does not accept. A war that leads to the destruction of the region that it was designed to save cannot be considered a triumph of diplomacy. American politics fragmented on this issue. Kosovo could be this generation's equivalent of Vietnam, a conflict that could split society and convulse us with self-righteousness. Meanwhile, the Balkans looks far from stable."

During an open discussion, "several participants thought that the panel was too gloomy. A Dane pointed out that the operation was a major success by the Alliance's own criteria, and that it had also garnered considerable legitimacy in the eyes of the public. It seemed perverse to complain that its soldiers were not killed in sufficient quantities. A British politician also thought the victory was worth celebrating. It was right to take on people like Saddam Hussein in the 1991 Iraq War and Milosevic in order to deter others. Kosovo involved questions of national interest as well as humanitarianism. And he insisted that getting rid of Milosevic should remain one of the clear aims of the alliance. . . . Others thought that a little gloom was indeed in order." A Greek member of the Group "warned of the depopulation of the region. An Austrian urged the international community to step in to deal with the problem of refugees . . . A Russian warned that, well meaning though it might have been, NATO's intervention would leave behind a huge number of long-term problems. These included resentment in Russia.

"The cost of rebuilding Kosovo and Serbia worried several speakers. One of the panelists pointed out that 70 percent of the targets had been infrastructure and predicted that reconstruction's costs would be gigantic. Another panelist doubted whether stability could be restored to the region without considerable investment—perhaps as much as $50 billion. A British politician wondered whether the alliance could hang together after the end of the war. He warned that there would be little popular enthusiasm for putting lots of resources into solving the region's gigantic problems.

"The idea that Kosovo had been the first post-nationalist war—and one that gave a huge boost to the ideal of European unification—came in for some heavy fire. A German argued that it was much too early to celebrate the birth of a new Europe. Had the war gone on, he said, the decision about whether to send in ground troops would have torn NATO apart. A Canadian pointed out that nothing would have been achieved without the United States. . . . A Portuguese worried about 'selective solidarity.' . . . A Russian argued that what they were witnessing was not so much the birth of the new world order as the collapse of the old one."

The first panelist argued against "the realpolitik school: that it is sometimes realistic to be moral and naive to be overcynical. . . . Everyone disapproved of massacres, and felt the question was how to prevent them in the first place. How did one persuade countries such as China, Russia and India that NATO's new mandate was not just a new version of colonialism? There were new dimensions to foreign policy, but they had to be looked at in a traditional framework."

In an address to NATO on June 22, 1999, that Bilderberg critics interpreted as an endorsement of a world government with NATO acting as global police force, President Clinton said that "if somebody comes after innocent citizens and tries to kill them en masse because of their race, their ethnic background or their religion, and if it's within our power to stop it, we will stop it."

Bilderberg watcher Jim Tucker noted in his book that a week later, *The Washington Post* columnist and Bilderberg attendee James Hoagland wrote that Clinton promises "a New World Order."

Speaking on November 4, 1999, on the subject of "An International Agenda for America," Clinton's national security advisor Samuel R. (Sandy) Berger told a meeting of the Bilderberg Steering Committee, "The coherent philosophy of a dominant minority, which sees international spending as inherently disconnected to America's interests, views most multilateral enterprises with suspicion and considers most difficult international endeavors, from supporting democracy in Russia to peace in the Balkans to growth in poor countries, as likely to fail and therefore not worth trying. That way of thinking has been with us in the United States for a long time. In recent times, we faced it in the 1950s when Senator Robert Taft challenged the internationalist wing of the Republican party, arguing that we should rely less on our allies and more on our own defenses. We saw it in the 1970s, when Congressional Democrats voted to bring our troops home from Europe, twisting legitimate concerns about Vietnam into a call to pull America out of the world."

In a speech that Bilderberg critics pointed to as endorsing "one-world government" in which NATO would be used to intervene in national affairs, as it did in Kosovo, Berger said, "America and its allies still face many dangers, some as old as ethnic conflict, some as new as cyberterrorism, some as fundamental as the risk that the democratic transitions which made this new era possible will not survive the strains of economic turmoil and political strife. That is why it is urgent that internationalists find common ground around a common agenda of our own. We must learn to recognize when our beliefs are being threatened. And we must defend them together. . . . We believe Americans benefit when nations coalesce to deter aggression, to resolve conflicts, to promote democracy, to open markets, to raise living standards, to prevent the spread of dangerous weapons, and to meet other dangers no nation can meet alone."

BILDERBERG 1999 MEETING ATTENDEES
(Source: Internet, "The 1999 Bilderberg Conference Attendees . . ." *Spotlight Newsletter #23*)

A—Austria	GB—England
B—Belgium	GR—Greece
BG—Bulgaria	H—Hungary
CDN—Canada	I—Italy
CH—Switzerland	ICE—Iceland
CZ—Czech Republic	INT—International
D—Germany	N—Norway
DK—Denmark	NL—Netherlands
E—Spain	P—Portugal
F—France	PL—Poland
FIN—Finland	RUS—Russia

S—Sweden   UKR—Ukraine
TR—Turkey   USA—United States

Agnelli, Umberto, president, IFIL Finanziaria di Partecipazioni
   S.p.A. (I)
Aguirre y Gil de Biedma, president of Spanish Senate (E)
Allaire, Paul A, president, Xerox Corporation (USA)
Amaral, Joaquim Ferreira do, member of Parliament (P)
Aslund, Anders, senior associate, Carnegie Endowment for
   International Peace (S)
Balsemao, Francisco Pinto, professor of communications science,
   New University, Lisbon (P)
Barnevik, Percy, chairman, investor AB (S)
Bayh, Evan, senator (D-Ind.) (USA)
Bernabe, Franco, managing director and CEO, Telegraph Group
   Limited (I)
Black, Conrad, chairman, Telegraph Group Limited (CDN)
Boucher, Eric Le, chief editor, *Le Monde* (F)
Boyd, Charles G., executive director of the National Security Study
   Group (USA)
Chastelain, John A. D. de, chairman, Independent International
   Commission on Decommissioning
Clarke, Kenneth, member of Parliament (GB)
Clement, Kristin, deputy director general, Confederation of Business
   and Industry (N)
Collomb, Bertrand, chairman and CEO, Lafarge (F)
Corzine, Jon, senator; ret. senior partner, Goldman Sachs & Co.
   (USA)
Cravinho, Joao, minister of Infrastructure, Planning and Territorial
   Administration (P)
David, George A., chairman of the board, Hellenic Bottling Company,
   SA (GR)

Dodd, Christopher J., senator (D-Conn.) (USA)

Donilon, Thomas E., attorney, O'Melveney and Meyers (USA)

Ercel, Gazi, governor, Central Bank of Turkey (TR)

Ergin, Sedat, Ankara bureau chief, Hurriyet (TR)

Feldstein, Martin S., president and CEO, National Bureau of Economic Research (USA)

Fischer, Stanley, director, IMF (INT)

Fresco, Paolo, chairman, Fiat S.p.A. (I)

Giavazzi, Francesco, professor of economics, Bocconi University, Milan (I)

Godsoe, Peter C., chairman and CEO, Bank of Nova Scotia (CDN)

Graham, Donald E., publisher, *The Washington Post* (USA)

Grave, Frank H. G., minister of defense (NL)

Grilo Eduardo Marcal, minister of education (P)

Hagel, Chuck, senator (R-Neb.) (USA)

Hedelius, Tom C., chairman, Svenska Handelsbanken (S)

Hegge, Per Egil, editor, *Aftenposten* (N)

Herrndorf, Peter A., former chairman and CEO, TV Ontario; senior fellow, University of Toronto (CDN)

Hoagland, Jim, associate editor, *The Washington Post* (USA)

Hoegh, Westye, chairman of the board, Leif Höegh & Co ASA (N)

Holbrooke, Richard C., ambassador to the UN designate (USA)

Huyghebaert, Jan, chairman, Almanij N.V. (B)

Ischinger, Wolfgang, state secretary, Ministry of Foreign Affairs (D)

Issing, Otmar, member of the Executive Board, European Central Bank (INT)

Jordan, Vernon E. Jr., senior partner, Akin, Gump, Strauss, Hauer & Feld LLP (USA)

Kamov, Nikolai, member of Parliament (BG)

Kirac, Suna, vice chairman of the board, Koc Holding AS (R)

Kissinger, Henry A., chairman, Kissinger Associates, Inc. (USA)

Kopper, Hilmard, chairman of the supervisory board, Deutsche
Bank (D)

Kranidiotis, Yannos, alternate minister of foreign affairs (GR)

Kravis, Marié-Josée, senior fellow, Hudson Institute (USA)

Leekanen, Erkki, member of FC (INT)

MacLaren, Roy, high commissioner for Canada in Britain (CDN)

MacMillan, Margaret O., editor, *International Journal* (CDN)

Mandelson, Peter, member of Parliament (GB)

Mathews, Jessica T., president, Carnegie Endowment for International
Peace (USA)

McDonough, William J., president, Federal Reserve Bank of New
York (USA)

McGinn, Richard A., chairman and CEO, Lucent Technologies
(USA)

Mello, Vasco de, vice chairman and CEO, Grupo Jose de Mello (P)

Mestrallet, Gerard A., chairman and CEO, Suez Lyonnaise des
Eaux (F)

Micklethwait, John, business editor, *The Economist* (GB)

Mityukov, Ihor, minister of finance (UKR)

Moisi, Dominique, director, IFRI INT (F)

Nass, Matthias, deputy editor, *Die Zeit* (D)

Netherlands, Her Queen Majesty the Queen (NL)

Oddsson, David, prime minister (ICE)

Olechowski, Andrzej, chairman, Central Europe Trust (PL)

Ollila, Jorman, president of the board and CEO, Nokia Corporation
(FIN)

Padoa-Schioppa, Tommaso, member of the Executive Board,
European Central Bank (INT)

Perger, Werner A., political correspondent, *Die Zeit* (D)

Porritt, Jonathon, program director, Forum for the Future (GB)

Profumo, Alessandro, CEO, Credito Italiano (I)

Pury, David de, chairman, de Pury Pictet Turrettini & Co, Ltd. (CH)

Richardson, Bill, secretary of energy (USA)

Rockefeller, David, chairman, Chase Manhattan Bank International (USA)

Rodriguez Inciarte, Matias, executive vice chairman, BSCH (E)

Rojas, Mauricio, associate professor of economic history, Lund University, director of Timbro's Center for Welfare Reform (S)

Roll, Eric, senior advisor, Warburg Dillon Read (GB)

Rosengren, Bjorn, minister for Industry, Employment and Communication (S)

Salgado, Ricardo E. S., president and CEO, Grupo Esprito Santo (P)

Sampaio, Jorge, president of Portugal (P)

Santos, Nicolau, editor-in-chief, *Expresso* (P)

Scharping, Rudolf, minister of defense (D)

Scheepbouwer, Ad J., chairman and CEO, TNT Poust Group (NL)

Schenz, Richard, CEO and chairman of the board of executive directors, Oesterreichische Kontrollbank AG (A)

Schempp, Jurgen E., chairman of the board of management, Daimler Chrysler (D)

Seidenfaden, Toger, editor-in-chief, *Politiken* AG (DK)

Shapiro, Robert B., chairman and CEO, Monsanto Company (USA)

Shevtsova, Lilia, Carnegie Moscow Center (RUS)

Silva, Artur Santos, president and CEO, BPI (P)

Solbes Mira, Pedro, member of Parliament, Socialist Party (E)

Surányi, György, president, National Bank of Hungary (H)

Taylor, J. Martin, formerly chief executive, Barclays PLC (GB)

Thoman, G. Richard, president and CEO, Xerox Corporation (USA)

Thornton, John L., president and co-CEO, Goldman Sachs Group, Inc. (USA)

Trenin, Dmitri V., deputy director, Carnegie Moscow Center (Rus)

Trichet, Jean-Claude, governor, Banque de France (F)

Tyson, Laura d'Andrea, professor, University of California, Berkeley (USA)

Vanhala, Matti, chairman of the board, Bank of Finland (F)

Vartia, Pentti, managing director, Research Institute of the Finnish Economy (F)

Vasela, Daniel L., chairman and CEO, Novartis AG (CH)

Veremis, Thanos M., professor of political history, University of Athens (GR)

Vranitzky, Franz, former federal chancellor (A)

Waal, Lodewijk J. de, chairman, Dutch Confederation of Trade Unions (NL)

Wolf, Martin, associate editor and economics commentator, *The Financial Times* (GB)

Wolfensohn, James D., president, The World Bank (INT/US)

Wolff von Amerongen, Otto, chairman and CEO, Otto Wolf GmbH (NT/US)

Wooldrige, Adrian D., foreign correspondent, *The Economist* (GB)

YŸcaoglu, Erkut, chairman, Tusiad (TR)

Zantovsky, Michael, chairman of the Committee on Foreign Affairs, Defense and Security, Czech State (CZ)

Zimmermann, Norbert, chairman, Berndorf AG (A)

• Eleven •

What About America?

Obtaining the official report of the 1999 Bilderberg meeting provided outsiders with their first concrete evidence of what transpired behind the closed doors at the Caesar Park Hotel Penha Longa in Sintra, Portugal, and proof that the Group was keenly interested in the political scene in the United States.

In his introduction to a discussion of the impending 2000 elections, the moderator argued that U.S. foreign policy was often influenced "by domestic concerns, with the main danger being an indifferent America, rather than an isolationist one."

The report noted, "This seemed to depress most of the subsequent speakers, who argued that on a variety of issues from free trade to China and Kosovo, American foreign policy seemed to lack leadership. And they looked for ways in which American politicians might be able to sell international issues to their constituents." The first panelist said the 2000 election was very important, not only because the United States would choose a president, but voters would decide control of the House of Representatives, and although the Democrats were unlikely to win the Senate, the GOP narrowed the gap considerably.

"Even the races for the State legislatures are interesting," he said, "because of redistricting. In California alone, the Democrats could pick up six seats in the House just by getting the right to draw the map.

The next speaker said, "Politics has always been a bizarre business. In 1991, George Bush's reelection was considered a formality. Seventeen months later, he was out of a job, having been comfortably beaten. At the moment few people expect foreign policy to play a strong role next year. They could be wrong. The last time foreign policy seemed significant was in the 1980 presidential race. But problems like Kosovo, the Middle East and the India-Pakistan squabble are not going to go away. And on the Republican side in particular, the expertise of the candidate may be judged on foreign policy. George W. Bush and John McCain look the two strongest candidates. There will come a moment when each candidate will be asked to define the national interest: to say what America's role in the world should be, and then to say how they will protect that interest. As long as the outside world is difficult and dangerous, it will affect domestic politics. Many Americans are beginning to realize that their livelihoods rely on events far away."

"Most of the participants seemed to agree with the first two panelists, rather than the third. They thought that foreign policy would play a relatively small role in the upcoming campaign. Instead the focus would be on domestic issues, such as education, healthcare, welfare and so on.

"The third panelist defended his position. Politics, he stated, is about relevance, and globalization is relevant. . . . Several participants seemed depressed about the relative unpopularity of free trade in American politics. One Canadian participant pointed to the failure to get trade on a fast track, and the lack of American leadership at the World Trade Organization (WTO).

"A panelist felt that politicians had failed to show the Americans where their long-term interests lay. . . . 'We have allowed the demagogues to fill the vacuum,' he complained, though he also stressed that politicians should do more for those who 'lost out because of free trade.'

"Although Russia briefly entered the discussion (one panelist argued that history would judge America poorly in its treatment of its former adversary), the two places deemed most likely to impact American foreign policy were China and Kosovo. . . . Whatever the result of the war in Kosovo, argued one panelist, the struggle still represented something of a failure for American foreign policy. It had never been properly explained to the American people. America had been given a second chance with Kosovo. It should not waste it. Several participants brought up the question of reconstruction."

The meeting then turned to "redesigning the international financial architecture." There was "a general sense that the global capital markets had run a little ahead of their regulators." Nobody disputed the idea that recent crises in emerging markets should be blamed primarily on the countries concerned. But many people thought that the recent series of dramatic upsets also seemed to highlight failings within the international financial system. The regulators present insisted that these failings were now being addressed. But many of the other participants remained skeptical.

In the first Bilderberg Group meeting where the Euro was a fact rather than a topic of a discussion, the conferees agreed that globalization of capital markets had happened much more quickly than globalization of regulatory systems. Advances in electronic data processing had combined with financial liberalization to make capital flows swifter and more uniform.

One participant expressed "grounds for being cynical about financial reform. Fear, greed and ignorance remained the main motors of markets. A leading central banker dismissed the attempts to rebuild the world's financial architecture as a little interior decoration. Globalization and the advance of information technology had upset the balance in financial markets. What was needed was not so much one massive redesign as a process of permanent adaptation.

"Several participants returned to the basic theme that the markets had globalized but the regulatory systems had not. Two European speakers thought the answer was to give a greater role to regional institutions, such as the European Union."

When the subject of post–Communism Russia was raised, a French participant argued that the West had "encouraged Russia to jump into a free-market system that it had taken forty years for Western Europe to embrace. He argued that perhaps 'we should recognize that we do not need a perfect world in order to do business.' Most participants were less sympathetic. A Swede pointed out that much of the money sent to Russia had been squandered. The state of the Russian coal industry, he felt, was not primarily a social problem, but a problem of organized crime. An American asked whether there would ever come a point at which the West would decide to stop lending money to Russia. One member said the West had a continuing interest in tying Russia into the international financial system."

Leadership of the next discussion, according to outsiders who claimed inside sources, was British Conservative Party member of Parliament and former Chancellor of the Exchequer Kenneth Clarke. Described as a friendly figure with "a relaxed charm appealing to the many voters who regard politicians as a breed of aliens," he was seen as "a heavyweight figure" in British politics. A cigar smoker who listed his hobbies as jazz, fast cars, and bird watching, he had been Health Secretary, Education Secretary, and home secretary before four successful years as chancellor of the exchequer. In October 1997, he joined the board of British American Tobacco. Since 1998, he had been the company's deputy chairman and senior independent nonexecutive director. Although he was a Tory Party leader, he favored closer ties to the EU and adoption of the Euro.

When a constituent, Mrs. Lynn Riley, of Chepstow, Monmouthshire, alleged in February 1997 that Clarke had failed to register a "free trip and accommodation he received from the Bilderberg Group," unlike Prime Minister Tony Blair who had attended the same meeting in Greece, the accusation was investigated.

Clarke said it was "his recollection that he paid his own airfare" but that his hotel bill was met. "He stated that he had since checked with conference organizers who confirmed that it was in accordance with their policy at the time for participants to meet their own travel costs; and that although they no longer kept complete records, they thought that the accommodation had been paid for by sponsors unknown, organized by their Greek members.

"Clarke subsequently explained that he and Blair considered that they were attending the conference as representatives of the Government." He told the investigator, "I was quite confident that I was at the time meeting the rules applying to Ministers."

The conference in question had taken place shortly before the House of Commons had approved a number of detailed changes to the rules on registration. "Before that date, members of Parliament were required to give details on their registration forms of 'overseas visits relating to or arising out of membership of the House where the cost of any such visit has not been wholly borne by the member or by public funds.' " A guide to the new rules, published in September 1993, provided, "Where only part of the costs was borne by an outside source (for example, the accommodation but not the cost of travel) those details should be stated briefly."

The investigator noted, "As Mr. Clarke correctly pointed out, neither he nor Mr. Blair registered their attendance at the conference on their return. Mr. Blair did so two years later in 1995, following a complaint that he had failed to register that visit, together with an earlier visit to Washington as a member of an All-Party Group. Mr. Clarke's recollection that he paid his own travel expenses is borne out by the conference organizers, and there is no reason to suppose that this was not the case. His accommodation expenses, on the other hand, do appear to have been met by his hosts. The Bilderberg Conference does not fall within a category which is exempt from registration and it follows that, in accordance with the rules both before and after June 1993, the partial benefit that he received ought to have been registered. I do however consider that any breach of the rules was of a relatively minor nature. Mr. Clarke saw himself as attending the conference as a representative of the Government, and had been careful to observe the requirement 'to ensure that no undue influence was involved.' "

As to the Bilderberg conference organizers paying for his accommodation, "the receipt of such a benefit could not realistically have been thought likely to influence his actions as a member of Parliament."

At the Bilderberg meeting in 1999, Clarke reportedly urged that the world should begin a transition to a global money system in three stages: the Euro, an Asian-Pacific currency, and the U.S. dollar in the Western Hemisphere, to be known as the "amerijo." Calling for a "world finance minister" at the United Nations," he predicted, "A generation from now, people will find it hard to believe that the world once had so many currencies."

Twelve

A New Millennium

With all the world's computers correctly registering the date, the Bilderberg Group met for the forty-seventh time on May 24, 2001, in the Hotel Stenungsbaden near the city of Gothenburg, Sweden. They were greeted by a bombshell lobbed by Margaret Thatcher.

The woman who had to be told by Denis Healey that getting a Bilderberg invitation meant she was expected to speak, and then had wowed them, was now a baroness and addressed as Lady Thatcher.

Three days before the Bilderberg conference, as Great Britain was at the beginning of an election called by Labour Party prime minister Tony Blair, she had said to the British Conservative Party rally at Plymouth, England, "The greatest issue in this election, indeed the greatest issue before our country, is whether Britain is to remain a free, independent, nation state. Or whether we are to be dissolved in a federal Europe. There are no half measures, no third ways, and no second chances. Too many powers have already passed from our Parliament to the [European Union] bureaucracy in Brussels. We must get them back. Above all, we must keep the pound. A country which loses the power to issue its own currency is a country which has given up the power to govern itself. Such a country is no longer free. And neither is it truly democratic, for its people can no longer determine their own future in national elections. To surrender the pound, to surrender our power of self-government, would betray all that past generations down the ages lived and died to defend. It would also be to turn our back on America, leader of the English-speaking peoples, to whom Europe, let's remember, also owes its freedom."

Called "Thatcher's revenge" on Bilderbergers who had turned against her, the speech was a powerful challenge to Tory Party leader William Hague's pledge to Labour Party prime minister Tony Blair to keep the issue of the Euro out of a general election scheduled for June 7, and the current session of Parliament would take no action on it. In response to the speech, Tony Blair gave one of his own in which he declared that support for replacing the pound for the Euro and for Britain to "share sovereignty" with the EU was "patriotic."

When Tory leader Hague said that "more and more rights of the British people are being signed away" to the EU, Labour Party officials accused him of "scare mongering."

Equally alarming to Bilderbergers as Thatcher's speech was an election in Italy that had given control of the Italian government to a conservative coalition headed by Silvio Berlusconi. Called "the biggest challenge yet to the young Euro currency" by *The Washington Post*, he made a fortune in real estate during the 1960s and then founded commercial television networks, becoming a billionaire as head of a media empire embracing television, advertising, film, and publishing. "Entering politics as a strong advocate of a market-driven economy, he had established the conservative Forza Italia party in 1994 and soon vaulted to prominence, largely through his excoriation of the corruption-tainted established parties and his ready access to publicity. In the 1994 parliamentary elections, his three-party right-wing coalition captured a majority, and he became premier. But by the end of the year, his coalition had collapsed and he resigned." Accused of corruption, he was convicted in 1997 and 1998 of financial crimes, but they were later overturned on appeal. In 2001 he was again elected premier and formed a right-wing coalition promising new jobs, increased pensions, public-works projects, and anticrime measures. Pledging dramatic tax cuts that the Bilderberg Group viewed as undermining the Euro, he was also denounced for his "anti-immigration views" that challenged the European Union concept of free movement across all national borders.

Noting that the Bilderberg 2001 agenda was expected to include EU enlargement, the bloc's military role, NATO's future, and developments in Russia and China, Reuters news agency reporter Peter Starck wrote that the regional daily newspaper *Göteborgs-Posten* had published a picture of "a 900-meter long metal fence erected around the" hotel. He also noted that anti-globalization demonstrators were expected to protest and that "local police see the event as a useful training exercise ahead of the mid-June European Union summit" in Gothenburg, about 30 miles to the south.

Aware that Swedes were curious about the mysterious arrangements at the posh hotel, "Bilderberg member Jacob Wallenberg, chairman of the board of commercial bank SEB and head of Sweden's influential Wallenberg family whose empire kept a finger in most big Swedish industries, played down the group's importance." He informed the daily newspaper *Dagens Nyheter*, "This is one of many meetings all over the world where decision makers get together." In a live studio interview about the Bilderberg Group on Sweden's TV4 television, Göran Greider, editor-in-chief of *Dala-Demokraten*, a regional Swedish daily, said, "Even though no formal decisions are made, this group, together with many others, has contributed to shaping the kind of capitalism we have today and cemented the world's leading business elites together." Gothenburg University political science professor Ulf Bjereld admitted that "secrecy is regarded as very provocative," but explained that "men in power talk towards consensus behind closed doors on timely issues on the political agenda."

Because the 2000 presidential election had put Republican George W. Bush into the White House, Democratic senator Christopher Dodd of Connecticut and newspaper tycoon Conrad Black led a 90-minute discussion on "the new U.S. administration" on Saturday, May 26. Bush was given high marks for promoting free trade agreements but all the speakers expressed disappointment that he rejected the Kyoto Treaty to control "global warming," defined as "one of the building blocks of Bilderberg's world government campaign." They also expressed their confidence that Bush could be "pressed into backing some kind of global warming pact."

U.S. assistant secretary of defense Richard Perle led a discussion on "European Security Defense Identity and Transatlantic Security." Born in New York City in 1941, Perle attended the University of Southern California, earning a B.A. in English in 1964. As an undergraduate he studied in Copenhagen at Denmark's International Study Program. He also studied at the London School of Economics and obtained an M.A. in political science from Princeton University in 1967. A Resident Fellow of the American Enterprise Institute for Public Policy Research since 1987, he directed a commission on "Future Defenses." A member of the Defense Policy Board since 1987, he became chairman in 2001. A frequent Bilderberg attendee, Perle had close business ties with Conrad Black, whose Hollinger International at one time owned more than four hundred daily and weekly newspapers in Canada, the United States, Britain, Israel, and Australia, including London's *The Daily Telegraph*, the *Chicago Sun-Times*, the *Sydney Morning Herald*, and *The Jerusalem Post*. As a director of Hollinger from June 1994, he was also co-chairman of Hollinger Digital, a media management and investment arm of Hollinger He had also been a director of *The Jerusalem Post*. He was on record as advocating "regime change" in Iraq by removal of dictator Saddam Hussein, by U.S. military force if necessary.

After Saturday lunch was served on the cruise ship *Erik*, the conference resumed with Henry Kissinger presiding over a discussion of "The Rise of China: Its Impact on Asia and the World." It was agreed that the United States must "remain engaged" in China. The importance of "opening Chinese markets" and smoothing China's path into the WTO was stressed. The closing session on Sunday, May 27, addressed what governments should do about food quality. The discussion was led by Franz Fischler, the representative of Austria in the EU. The consensus was that a United Nations bureaucracy must be established to make certain the global population has a healthy diet.

As Bilderbergers headed to their respective countries, "an inside source" confided to *Spotlight* reporter Jim Tucker, "Bilderberg is really dazed. They thought by now the EU would be a full superstate with nation-states obsolete."

When the Group gathered for its 2002 meeting, their organization that had been born during the Cold War and saw Joseph Retinger's dream of a European Union nearly realized suddenly faced not only a threat to continental solidarity but a peril to thousands of years of Western society and two millennia of Christian civilization. Seven months after two Islamic terrorist attacks destroyed New York's World Trade Center and badly damaged the Pentagon, killing nearly three thousand Americans, the Bilderbergers convened in the Washington, DC, suburb of Chantilly, Virginia. As they met at the plush Westfields Marriott hotel from May 30 to June 3, 2002, American troops had been at war in Afghanistan to depose the Taliban government and root out the terrorist bases of Osama bin Laden's Al Qaeda where the attacks on the Twin Towers and the Pentagon on September 11, 2001, had been planned and the hijackers had trained.

The official press release for the 2002 Bilderberg meeting said the conference would discuss terrorism, trade, post-crisis reconstruction, Middle East, civil liberties, U.S. foreign policy, "Extreme Right," world economy, and corporate governance.

In 2003, the Group met in mid-May at the Trianon Palace Hotel in Versailles, France, and heard a welcoming speech by President Jacques Chirac. As usual, the hotel was closed to the public and all non-Bilderberg guests had to check out. Part-time employees were sent home. The ones who remained were told that they would be fired if caught revealing anything about the meeting. Armed guards isolated the hotel.

According to *Asia Times* reporter Pepe Escobar, the customary amity between U.S. and European participants had fallen victim to the new global crisis centered around the Middle East, which replaced the crisis evolving around the Cold War. Citing "a banking source in the City of London connected to Versailles," Escobar wrote that American and Europeans "have not exactly managed to control their split over the American invasion and occupation of Iraq, as well as over Israeli prime minister Ariel Sharon's hard-line policy against the Palestinians."

The item continued, "American imperial adventures are usually rehearsed at Bilderberg meetings. Europe's elite were opposed to an American invasion of Iraq since the 2002 Bilderberg meeting in Chantilly, Virginia. . . . Europe's elite, according to those close to Bilderberg, are suspicious that the United States does not need or even want a stable, legitimate central government in Iraq. When that happens, there will be no reason for the United States to remain in the country. Europe's elite see the United States . . . establishing a long-term military presence and getting the oil flowing again under American control."

The Group also struggled to forge a consensus on the necessity of an EU army totally independent of NATO. Noting that some Europeans suggested a separate force, but controlled by NATO, and Americans argued that a separate EU force would supplant NATO, which was no longer confined to the defense of Europe and could go anywhere in the world, directed or not by the United Nations Security Council.

According to some Bilderberg observers, NATO would eventually be converted into a UN military force, but in a manner to deceive Americans who were wary of the United Nations. In this scheme, the term "NATO" must always be used. The Bilderbergers reasoned that the American public was already "propagandized to love NATO," but most had come to distrust and despise the UN. By invoking NATO, the American people would allow foreign commanders to be put in charge of U.S. fighting forces. In actuality, NATO would become the enforcement arm of the United Nations, and in effect the police of the global government that was the ultimate goal of the Bilderberg Group.

Although NATO was created to defend Western Europe from the Soviet Union, with the United States providing the military muscle, after the end of the Cold War, its role was expanded in the Kosovo war to one of intervention. As Javier Solana wrote in the journal *Foreign Affairs*, "NATO's Kosovo operation was a major challenge in the history of the Atlantic alliance. For the first time, a defensive alliance launched a military campaign to avoid a humanitarian tragedy outside its own borders. For the first time, an alliance of sovereign nations fought not to conquer or preserve territory but to protect the values on which the alliance was founded."

Expanding its reach outside Europe, NATO deployed more than 5,200 troops to Afghanistan to assist the Afghan government "in extending and exercising its authority and influence across the country, creating the conditions for stabilization and reconstruction." Said NATO secretary general Jaap de Hoop Scheffer, "This is one of the most challenging tasks NATO has ever taken on, but it is a critical contribution to international security."

The Alliance's aim, said a NATO publication, was to "help establish the conditions in which Afghanistan can enjoy, after decades of conflict, destruction and poverty, a representative government and self-sustaining peace and security." NATO's contribution was seen as "a test of legitimacy for future NATO missions."

The U.S. Ambassador to NATO, Victoria Nuland, stated, "If we can't do missions like that of Afghanistan, then we can't do our overall mission."

Taking a wary position, American columnist John F. McManus wrote, "Afghanistan is immensely distant from what has always been known as the North Atlantic region. Yet United States, and other coalition forces in Afghanistan are now serving under the auspices of

NATO. That transfer of power also placed our Afghanistan military operations under UN command since NATO has always been a UN subsidiary. Hence, once again, NATO is being employed as the UN's military arm."

At a conference in Munich, Germany, on February 13, 2005, Senator Hillary Clinton said, "In the post–Cold War world, NATO, and other multinational military forces, can and should play important roles in peacekeeping operations in support of UN mandates."

In December 1993, a *Los Angeles Times* poll asked, "Should the United States try to use force only in concert with the UN, or should the United States use force in our own national interest regardless of the UN?" Fifty-nine percent said the United States should act only with the UN in using force, while just 31 percent said the United States should use force to pursue national interests. In a December 1992 *Newsweek* poll, 87 percent agreed that "the United Stated should commit its troops only as part of a UN operation."

Henry Kissinger was reported to have said in an address to the Bilderberger meeting at Évian, France, on May 21, 1992, "Today Americans would be outraged if UN troops entered Los Angeles to restore order; tomorrow they will be grateful. This is especially true if they were told there was an outside threat from beyond whether real or promulgated that threatened our very existence. It is then that all peoples of the world will pledge with world leaders to deliver them from this evil. The one thing every man fears is the unknown. When presented with this scenario, individual rights will be willingly relinquished for the guarantee of their well-being granted to them by their world government."

Thirteen

OFF THE RECORD

Were it not for reports by Jim Tucker, Daniel Estulin, Tony Gosling, Alex Jones, and a few others in Europe, very little information about the Bilderberg Group would be known. Since the first meeting in 1954, dozens of journalists who attended have scrupulously abided by the secrecy rule. "Mainstream news organizations boastful about their no-holds barred investigative exploits," Estulin noted, "have been strangely reluctant to lift the blackout curtain." Tucker wrote, "Bilderberg has, at one time or another, had representatives of all major U.S. newspapers and network news outlets attend. They do so on their promise to report nothing. This is how Bilderberg keeps its news blackout virtually complete in the United States."

A review of *The New York Times* archives found that since the start of the Group in 1954, there were twenty-three "Bilderberg" mentions. Seven of them dealt with the death of Bernhard or his involvement in the Lockheed scandal. Six items referred to Bilderberg in a tangential way. One was a profile of Vernon Jordan. Only one story dealt with a particular meeting. It was held in Stresa, Italy, in 2004. Under the headline "Conspiracy Theorists Unite; A Secret Conference Thought to Rule the World," reporters Alan Cowell and David M. Halbfinger wrote, "The meetings are hardly a monument to transparency."

Although neither reporter attended the meeting, they noted that a speech by Senator John Edwards was well received and that it was "one reason for his selection as John Kerry's vice-presidential running mate." Suspicions that Bilderberg was an elite conspiracy to run the world were dismissed. "The guest list and membership," wrote Cowell and Halbfinger, "would more or less overlap with the 'Wanted' posters of anti-globalization protestors."

Most likely to attract press attention to Bilderberg is a discovery of the attendance at a meeting by a government official. On June 12, 2006, *The New York Sun* instructed, "Don't bother asking Governor [George] Pataki what he was up to over the weekend. It's a secret, and he can't tell you."

Staff reporter Jacob Gershman wrote, "After wrapping up the usual state business, Mr. Pataki flew to Canada to participate in the annual conclave of the Bilderberg Group, a clandestine club of the world's business and political elite that has been likened to a shadow government and has been said to shape global events."

Although Pataki's spokesman, David Catalfamo, did not return phone calls and e-mails seeking comment on the governor's participation, the Bilderberger who invited him spoke to the *Sun* reporter. Richard Perle said, "I think he's intelligent and thoughtful, sort of the person who would go and spend a weekend listening to a discussion of a broad range of policy issues."

Perle noted that Pataki was the only American governor at the meeting and the only politician known to be considering a presidential run in 2008.

Noting that the Bilderberg discussions were off the record, and nobody on the inside was allowed to talk about it with outsiders, *Sun* reporter Gershman wrote, "Mr. Pataki could assume that whatever happened in Ottawa would stay in Ottawa."

Among newsmen who were said to have attended Bilderberg meetings were James Hoagland (a regular) and Charles Krauthammer, both columnists for *The Washington* Post; Jean de Belot, editor of the French newspaper *le Figaro;* Paul Gigot, editorial page editor of *The Wall Street Journal;* Bill Kristol of *The Weekly Standard;* Charlie Rose, host of a nightly eponymous interview show on PBS; and Kenneth Whyte of Canada, editor of *The National Post.* Others of the Fourth Estate who were reported to have attended Bilderberg Group meetings were News Corporation and Fox News Channel founder Rupert Murdoch; Donald E. Graham, chairman of the board of *The Washington Post* Company; Lesley Stahl of *60 Minutes,* Peter Jennings of ABC News; Andrea Mitchell, NBC News; Bill Moyers of PBS; columnist George Will; and William F. Buckley, Jr., founder of *National Review.*

Requests by this author via e-mail to several Washington and New York journalists who had attended Group meetings for either a comment by return e-mail or an opportunity to interview them on their Bilderberg experience for this book went unanswered.

Arguably the most controversial Bilderberger from the ranks of the press was Conrad Black. The owner of a string of newspapers around the world, he was born in Montreal to a wealthy family; son of the president of Canadian Breweries, an international brewing conglomerate; and related to the founder of the Great-West Life Assurance Company and an early co-owner of *The Daily Telegraph,* Black graduated from a small private school in Toronto. He earned a law degree at Université Laval and a master of arts degree in history at McGill University. His thesis, later published as a biography, was on the Quebec premier Maurice Duplessis. In 1966, he bought his first newspaper, *Eastern Townships Advertiser,* in Quebec. Following the foundation, as an investment vehicle, of the Ravelston Corporation by the Black family in 1969, Black, together with friends David Radler and Peter G. White, purchased and operated the *Sherbrooke Record,* a small English language daily in Sherbrooke, Quebec. In 1971, the three formed Sterling Newspapers Limited, a holding company that would acquire several other small Canadian regional newspapers.

When Black's father died in 1976, he left him and older brother,

Montegu, a 22.4 percent stake in Ravelston, which by then owned 61 percent voting control of Argus Corporation, an influential holding company in Canada. Argus exercised control of Canadian corporations, including Canadian Breweries Limited, Dominion Stores, Hollinger Mines, and Standard Broadcasting, and others.

In 1985, Andrew Knight, then editor of *The Economist*, asked Black to invest in the ailing Telegraph Group. By this investment, Black made his first entry into British press ownership. Five years following, he bought *The Jerusalem Post*, and subsequently fired the majority of its staff. By 1990, his companies ran over four hundred newspaper titles in North America, the preponderance of them small community papers. Hollinger bought a minority stake in the Southam newspaper chain in 1993 and acquired the *Chicago Sun-Times* in 1994.

In 1996, Barbara Leiterman of Fairness and Accuracy in Media (FAIR) wrote, "There's a new player among the global media moguls, and his name is Conrad Black." His company, Hollinger International, was then the third largest newspaper chain in the Western world, after Gannett and Rupert Murdoch's News Corporation, with a combined circulation exceeding 10 million. "Black owns 650 dailies and weeklies around the world, including *The Jerusalem Post*, *The Daily Telegraph* in London, the *Sydney Morning Herald*, and the *Chicago Sun-Times*. He began this media empire by buying up small papers in his native Canada" to control "42 percent of Canada's daily circulation and most of the large papers outside of Toronto."

According to David Robinson, research director at the Council of Canadians, these assets include 70 percent of Ontario's newspapers, almost every paper in British Columbia, and all the papers in Newfoundland, Prince Edward Island, and Saskatchewan. In the "Moneybox" column of *Slate* Magazine, Daniel Gross wrote that Black "imagined himself to be not merely a peddler of newspapers, but a Metternich in the boardroom" and that owning a media company was an excuse to muse over the Treaty of Vienna with board members like Henry

Kissinger." It was at a Bilderberg meeting that Black commenced a relationship with Richard Perle, and Perle quickly became part of Black's inner circle, serving on Hollinger's executive committee.

As an author, Black published a memoir, *Conrad Black: A Life in Progress*, in 1993; a biography, *Franklin Delano Roosevelt: Champion of Freedom*, in 2003, and *The Invincible Quest: The Life of Richard Milhous Nixon*, in 2007.

In the *New York Post* on January 5, 2004, Richard Wolff wrote of Black's publishing enterprises and Bilderberg membership, "Stature is what he's sought: standing, significance, importance—especially among other men of standing, significance, and importance. Black has seemed not much interested in influencing the views of the masses (nor has he appeared to have much talent for clever or commercial propaganda), but rather those of other men of influence. He has been one of the world's great patrons of the neoconservative view (Euro-skeptical, pro-Israel, free market), keeping such like-minded acolytes (or is he their acolyte?) as Henry Kissinger, Richard Perle, William Buckley, and George Will on his company's various and shadowy payrolls."

Black said in *A Life in Progress*, "It was from Bilderberg that our company's eventual vocation as an international newspaper organization arose. Not having very satisfactory recollections of schooldays, nor being a very enthusiastic or observant university alumnus, Bilderberg has been the closest I have known to that sort of comaraderie. The animated social sessions, as much as the cut and thrust on the principal strategic and economic issues faced by the Atlantic community, have given me, and many other regular participants, a powerful and entirely agreeable sense of community with some very talented and prominent people. After 1986, I became the co-leader of the Canadian group and effectively chose most of the Canadian participants [in Bilderberg]."

When the Group chose to meet in Canada, *The Toronto Star*, one of the few remaining independent newspapers in the country, ran a front-page story under the headline "Black Plays Host to World Leaders." The paper's business reporter, John Deverell, noted that among the more than one hundred attendees "from around the world were U.S. defense secretary William Perry, Canadian prime minister Jean Chrétien, Henry Kissinger, the queens of Netherlands and Spain, as well as other business, political and academic elite."

In addition to being a Bilderberger, Black was a member of Sotheby's board of directors, the Council on Foreign Relations' International Advisory Board, the Fraser Institute board of trustees, the Institute for International Economics board of directors, and the Richard Nixon Center board of directors.

All this came crashing down in December 2007 when Black was convicted of defrauding stockholders of newspaper conglomerate Hollinger International. Sentenced to six and a half years in federal prison, he had skimmed millions of dollars to finance his lavish lifestyle and for the benefit of men he had met through the Bilderberg Group.

"The press lord who hoped to dominate the worlds of journalism, high society, high finance and aristocracy," said the *New York Post*, owned by Black's competitor in the world of journalism, Rupert Murdoch, had pilfered funds at shareholders' expense to finance "three or four mansions, yachts, jet planes, flights to places like Bora Bora, an apartment swap in New York, million-dollar decorators, jewelry, and high-end clothes for Mrs. Black."

A story in *The New York Times* on December 22, 2003, that included a rare mention of Bilderberg carried the headline: FRIENDSHIP AND BUSINESS BLUR IN THE WORLD OF A MEDIA BARON. Reporters Jacques Steinberg and Geraldine Fabrikant wrote, "On the dust jacket of his recently published biography of Franklin D. Roosevelt, Conrad M. Black, the embattled media magnate, collected laudatory blurbs from an impressive set of conservative thinkers. Henry A. Kissinger writes, 'No biography of Roosevelt is more thoughtful and readable.' The columnist George F. Will calls the book a 'delight to read.'

And William F. Buckley, Jr., commends the biography as 'a learned volume on FDR by a vital critical mind.' What the blurbs did not mention was that each man was praising the work of a sometime boss."

Unrecognized by the *Times* was that all were Bildebergers.

"During the 1990s, Black had appointed all three to an informal international board of advisers of Hollinger International. For showing up once a year with Lord Black to debate the world's problems, each of Black's Bilderberg associates was typically paid about $25,000 a year. . . . The advisory board was one example of how friendships with the rich and often politically influential overlapped with business in Lord Black's world. The board became a who's who of mostly conservative thinkers and politicians that included Margaret Thatcher, Valéry Giscard d'Estaing, Zbigniew Brzezinski, Richard N. Perle, and the former head of Archer Daniels Midland, Dwayne O. Andreas."

Not reported by *The Times* was that all had attended Bilderberg meetings.

The Times item asserted that "Black had enjoyed more than just conversation from the advisers Hollinger paid for." It noted that Will and Buckley had "written positively about Black" in their columns, "without mentioning their business dealings or their Bilderberg connection." "The seemingly porous boundary" among Black's social, political, and business lives, wrote Steinberg and Fabrikant, which was reflected in the composition of the Hollinger board, had been "thrown into relief" by the investigation of Black's business affairs. They noted that Henry Kissinger, Perle, and Andreas had served as directors at times when they were also getting paid by the company for their advice to Black. "A closer look at the members of Lord Black's inner circle shed light not just on board oversight," *The Times* article continued, but also on how he managed to transform himself as Hollinger grew from an obscure Canadian company that owned mines and supermarkets into the owner of more than a hundred daily newspapers, including *The Daily Telegraph* in London, *The Jerusalem Post*, and the *Chicago Sun-Times*. In the process,

Lord Black became a throwback press baron who lived lavishly on Park Avenue, in Palm Beach and in London and was at ease in the most prominent salons in the world."

Noting that Brzezinski said he had first met Black at one of several international conferences that they frequented, *The Times* stated, "One is known as Bilderberg Group, a conclave of business and political leaders from North America and Europe that meets each year for discussions that are off the record."

The rare reference to Bilderberg was in keeping with an apparent *Times* aversion to running stories about the Bilderberg Group. The only other reference in the story written by Steinberg and Fabrikant was to *Shades of Black*, a biography of Black by Richard Siklos, a former reporter for *Business Week* and *The Financial Post*, a Toronto business newspaper. In the early 1990s, said Siklos, Black decided to form "a miniature Bilderberg of his own" by creating a board to advise the Hollinger executives on international affairs. "In its earliest incarnations," Siklos wrote, "the advisory board included Mr. Kissinger, Mr. Perle and Mr. Brzezinsk; as well as Paul A. Volcker, the former head of the Federal Reserve; Chaim Herzog, the former president of Israel . . . ; and Lady Thatcher. They were joined by others, including Mr. Will and Mr. Buckley."

Following the Bilderberg meetings' pattern "at the advisory meetings, each participant was assigned a topic. At times, . . . the conversations extended to a second day," but Buckley was reported to have felt that although these conversations at the advisory meetings could be illuminating, he was hard pressed to find an example of how the sessions were of assistance to Hollinger. In his syndicated column, Will recounted observations that Black had made in a London speech defending the Bush administration's stance on Iraq. Will wrote, "Into this welter of foolishness has waded Conrad Black, a British citizen and member of the House of Lords who is a proprietor of many newspapers."

When Will was asked if he should have told his readers of the payments he received from Hollinger, Will said, "My business is my business. Got it?"

Similarly, in a column published in *The National Review* in 2002, editor William F. Buckley, Jr., wrote of attending a dinner at Black's home in London and stated that Black and his wife, Barbara Amiel, were among his "five closest friends in the entire world." Asked later why he had not mentioned his payments from Hollinger, Buckley said, "I didn't think that had any bearing whatsoever." To underscore that he did not feel beholden to Black, Buckley mentioned a "withering review" of Black's Roosevelt biography that had appeared in *The National Review*.

Aside from "some good press," said Steinberg and Fabrikant, there had been "more tangible benefits" for both Black and people who associated with him. In addition to serving on the Hollinger board, Richard Perle was chairman or co-chairman of Hollinger Digital, a unit of the parent company, and was paid more than $300,000 a year and $2 million in bonuses over part of that period, according to someone "with knowledge of the company." And Trireme, a venture capital firm partly managed by Perle and advised by Black, received a $2.5 million investment from Hollinger, according to company filings reported in *The Wall Street Journal*. Hollinger also gave about $200,000 a year to *The National Interest*, a foreign affairs publication where Black and Kissinger were co-chairmen of the editorial board, of which Perle was a member.

"I think Conrad did these things less for the bottom line than to create the aura that the group gave him," said Peter Munk, the founder and chairman of Barrick Gold, and someone who briefly served on the Hollinger board. "He reveled in that aura."

American journalists for whom reveling in an aura surrounding the world's financial and political movers and shakers might or might not have been a reason to attend Bilderberg have been scrupulous in adhering to the Bilderberg Group pledge of being silent about their attendance at meetings and what they heard. Consequently, those who look at the Bilderberg Group with suspicion believe that because none of these newsmen report on the meetings, it constitutes proof that they are participants in a conspiracy to rule the world.

Of the Bilderberg meeting in Instanbul, Turkey, in 2007, Paul Joseph Wilson of the Internet *Prison Planet* wrote, "Number of mainstream U.S. news outlets that reported on Paris Hilton over the past week: 10,000 plus. Number of mainstream U.S. news outlets that reported on a meeting of nearly 200 of the world's most powerful people this past weekend; Less than a handful. The Bilderberg Group meeting, an annual conference at which the consensus for future global policy is provably manifested, again passed by with barely a mention on behalf of America's corporate media."

Wilson added, "*The Dallas Morning News* carried a single article about Texas governor Perry's visit, a story that was subsequently picked up in brief blurbs by a couple of local Texas television news affiliates and a few bylines on page 30 of a couple of papers in the lone star state. Apart from that, nothing, absolutely nothing about a confab of the most powerful and influential people on the planet. Nothing in *The New York Times* and nothing in *The Washington Post* or *The Wall Street Journal*, both of which were represented at the meeting. Nothing in *Le Figaro* of France or the *Financial Times* of London, who also were both represented by chief editors."

Governor Perry made no secret of his attendance. On May 31, 2007, Christy Hoppe wrote in *The Dallas Morning News* that the governor's press secretary announced that Perry was invited to attend and speak about state-federal relations. Black dismissed conspiracy theories by joking that Perry was "looking forward to learning the secret handshake." He said that Perry was paying for the trip and his hotel accommodation from campaign contributions from his "Texans for Rick Perry" committee. He noted that the governor was going because he was invited and "looks forward to talking to them about the system of federalism here in the United States." Regarding the secrecy surrounding the event, the press secretary said, "It's their conference, and I suppose they can run it anyway they want. The governor was honored that they would ask him to come speak on the American experience, and he's happy to do it."

Presented with the proposition of a journalistic blackout as part of a conspiracy, a famous television journalist who spoke only after being promised anonymity scoffingly replied, "That is pure bullshit! I attend Bilderberg meetings because I get a long weekend at a five-star hotel in a very pleasant place, removed from the pressures of deadlines, in the company of very smart men. For a couple of days, I can relax and at the same time learn points of view on vital issues that are useful to me both personally and professionally. It costs me no more than an ordinary three-day holiday, but with nobody bothering me to ask for an autograph!"

While almost nothing about the Bilderberg Group has appeared in the newspapers and magazines of the world, or on television, Bilderbergers have attracted the attention of scores, if not hundreds, of Internet sites and "bloggers." A Google search for "Bilderberg" resulted in 1,960,000 items. A Yahoo search provided 4,790,000. Among the sites were YouTube, SourceWatch, Crystallinks, Prisonplanet, Infowars, Propagandatrix, Likeleak, Worldpress, and Indymedia. Almost all depicted the Group as a suspicious, conspiratorial organization.

A rare dissent was provided by the Anti-Defamation League. Its site noted, "ADL has received inquiries about conspiracy theories regarding the Bilderberg group, a legitimate business entity with ties to Europe and America. The following information from the ADL's Civil Rights Information Center debunks a recurring myth, circulated via the Internet, that the group is part of a conspiracy to promote a 'new world order' under their control."

The ADL site said, "The Bilderberg group is an actual, legitimate entity whose members consist of approximately 100 influential European and American figures in politics, business and academia who meet annually to discuss and advocate political, diplomatic and economic policies."

It continued, "Various far-right extremists and conspiracy theorists, however, charge that the group is a shadowy force seeking to control world events, exerting allegedly dominating powers of international influence to promote a 'new world order' under their control. The extremists claim that presidential candidates of both major U.S. political parties are controlled by the Bilderberg group; among those often mentioned in such conspiracy-oriented propaganda are David Rockefeller, the Clintons and Henry Kissinger."

In *The True Story of the Bilderberg Group*, Daniel Estulin stated that Anthony Holder, a former UN correspondent for the London *Economist* had stated, "The Bilderbergers have been removed from our assignment list years ago."

Estulin also quoted William Glasgow, a senior writer responsible for covering international organizations for *Business Week*. He was reported to have said, "We are barely aware of the Bilderbergers' existence and we don't report on their activities. One cannot help but be a little suspicious when priorities for the future of mankind are being considered by those who have real influence over that future, in total secret."

Discerning an interlocking of Bilderberg members and executives of major American communications corporations, broadcast and cable networks, and newspapers and magazines, Estulin wrote, "The ideas and policies that come out of the Bilderberg annual meetings are used to generate news in the leading periodicals and news groups of the world."

Among stories of alleged Bilderberg censorship circulated by Bilderberg watchers is the case of G. Gordon Tether. For years the writer of a prestigious and influential column for *The Financial Times of London*, he said in his May 6, 1975, column, "If the Bilderberg Group is not a conspiracy of some sort, it is conducted in such a way as to give a remarkably good imitation of one."

According to Bilderberg observers, this was Tether's last reference to the Group that appeared. As a Bilderberg watcher put it, "He continued to write articles mentioning the Group, but editorial management barred every single one of them from publication. After battling this censorship for two years, Tether was finally dismissed by *The Financial Times*."

British "freelance journalist Campbell Thomas was also said to have seen the ugly side of Bilderberg secrecy when he attempted to cover the 1998 conference for *The Daily Mail*." As a newsman "with eight years' experience, he happened to be a special constable as well. Like other journalists at the conference, he remained outside the police security ring surrounding the Turnberry Hotel" in Scotland. "Hoping to get neighbors' reactions to the conference, he entered a block of flats through an open door about five hundred yards away. At the first door he knocked on, the young woman who answered informed Thomas that he was in the hotel's staff quarters, and that he should not be there. He left immediately. A short while later, two Strathclyde police officers approached Thomas and told him that he was being detained. Even though he showed the policemen his special constable identity card, he was handcuffed and kept in custody for eight hours."

As the time for the 2008 meeting drew near, Bilderberg watchers pondered where it would be held. A blogger in Ireland suggested the Emerald Isle, Portugal, and France. He wrote, "Any ideas? They were in Portugal once in 1999 and haven't returned since. The 2004 meeting was significant for them in that the 3 Portugese delegates went on to get prominent positions in their fields. And in 2007 we have 3 prominent Portugese delegates at the Bilderberg meeting. If they weren't there in the intervening years, then this may be a good sign. However, I guess we won't really know until someone leaks it in a newspaper report of some description. It's still likely to be in Europe considering they were in Canada in 2006 and tend to only return to the North American continent cyclically every few years. Please keep your eyes peeled for any articles."

Late in February, a blogger asked, "Any ideas where the 'gang' is meeting this year? haven't heard anything concrete this year for the 2008 Bilderberg group meeting. Does anyone have any more up to date information? Last year was Turkey and the year before was Ottawa."

One reply said, "No, but it is getting harder for them to hide every year. Thanks to some brave guys, who have got them cornered."

Another ventured, "Belize. The coke is free from patent infringements there."

"Ireland or France seems to be the best guesses," said a third, "but who knows for sure. I didn't get my invite yet."

In March 2008, based on television news stories, a Dutch Bilderberg watcher reported, "The pro-U.S. prime minister Jan Peter Balkenende, and the likewise compliant and collaborating minister of foreign affairs, Maxime Verhagen, will visit President George Bush in Washington next June 5, and thereafter attend the annual Bilderberg conference. In the Dutch TV story, it's confirmed that both will visit President Bush. Thereafter, the story said, Balkenende would take part in the Bilderberg conference in the United States. Some further research shows that it is highly probable that Holland's PM Balkenende and Minister Verhagen will attend this annual Bilderberg conference in Chantilly, Virginia, close to Dulles International Airport. It was held there six years ago as well, conference center of the Westfields Marriott hotel."

In early May 2008, came a report from Greece that the Group would meet in the resort town of Vouliagmeni.

This news was founded on a supposed sighting of Henry Kissinger. On May 13, Tony Gosling reported, "Well the old tricksters did it this year. They evaded all our efforts to track them down to a precise date and venue. There has been a lot of Bilderberg searching activity, including examination of Bilderbergers' schedules, checking of hotels but no 100% definite answer. . . . The trouble is that this year particularly all key Bilderberg people have been keeping very quiet about their future plans. In past years they have been relatively open about where they were planning to be and it's then quite a simple matter to identify gaps in the schedules of, say the boss of the European Central Bank and the Queen of the Netherlands, that coincide."

On May 14, an observer noted, "A sole report from a small Greek media outlet indicates that the annual Bilderberg meeting took place undetected over the weekend in Athens, Greece, amidst a complete media lockdown."

In late May, Gosling confirmed the Group would be meeting at Chantilly from June 5 to June 9 and announced that he would be there to greet them.

A May 28, 2008, blogger wrote, "I think they're just very greedy humans engaged in high level cronyism, working together to ensure that the table stays tilted their way no matter what comes. I hope they choke on their freaking hors d'oeuvres [and] realize that the only thing we leave this life with is integrity or lack of it and start thinking about the welfare of the whole and all start cleansing diets and give their yachts to Greenpeace and put all their assets to use helping to make the world a better place."

On June 5, a blogger reported that an "employee working for Apple Computers sent an e-mail to the website "Infowars" reporting that the department of justice had placed an order for 125 ipods with "Bilderberg 2008" engraved on the back shipping to Chantilly "at American taxpayer expense." According to this anonymous source, the "DOJ is freaking out because the order will arrive late."

On June 5, the website Disinformation stated, "Spooks, FBI agents and cops have descended on the Westfields Marriott hotel in Chantilly, Virginia, to scrutinize Jim Tucker and Alex Jones as the 2008 Bilderberg meeting gets underway today without even being mentioned in the American corporate media."

As usual, the official Bilderberg press release gave only basic facts. Issued on June 6, it stated, "The 56th Bilderberg Meeting will be held in Chantilly, Virginia, USA 5–8 June 2008. The Conference will deal mainly with a nuclear free world, cyber terrorism, Africa, Russia, finance, protectionism, US-EU relations, Afghanistan and Pakistan, Islam and Iran. Approximately 140 participants will attend, of whom about two thirds come from Europe and the balance from North America. About one third is from government and politics, and two thirds are from finance, industry, labor, education and communications. The meeting is private in order to encourage frank and open discussion."

The remainder of the press release was the same as all previous notices, giving a brief history of the Group, stating the meeting was private, that after the meetings there would be no press conference, and a list of participants was available upon request by telephone. Frustrated by the news blackouts, and believing that members of the mainstream press are part of the conspiracy of silence, Bilderberg watchers assert that after a recent Bilderberg meeting, David Rockefeller was reported to have said, "We are grateful to *The Washington Post, The New York Times, Time* magazine, and other great publications whose directors have attended our meetings and respected their promises of discretion for almost forty years. . . . It would have been impossible for us to develop our plan for the world if we had been subject to the bright lights of publicity during these years. But, the world is now more sophisticated and prepared to march towards a world government."

• Fourteen •

BILDERBERG BROTHERS

In the twenty-seventh chapter of his memoirs titled *Proud International-ist*, David Rockefeller acknowledged allegations that he was accused of conspiring with others around the world to build a more integrated global political and economic structure. "If that's the charge," he said, "I stand guilty and I am proud of it."

He continued that his accusers, including Bilderberg critics, believed in conspiracies, and that one of the most enduring supposed plots is that a secret group of international bankers and capitalists, and their minions, control the world's economy.

Because of his name and prominence as the head of the Chase Bank for many years, he said, "I have earned the distinction of 'conspirator in chief.'"

Waving that banner, he wrote "that the United States cannot escape from its global responsibilities. Today's world cries out for leadership," and America must provide it because in the twenty-first century there can be no place for isolationists.

Critics of Bilderberg note that five years before Rockefeller became a founder of the Bilderberg Group, he had been elected to membership in the Council of Foreign Relations (CFR). In concept and goals, it has been regarded as the Group's older brother. But the lineage began in the aftermath of World War I.

Established in New York on July 29, 1921, with 108 founding members, including Elihu Root as a leading member and John W. Davis, the chief counsel for J. P. Morgan & Co. and former solicitor general for President Wilson, as its founding president. (Davis was to become Democratic presidential candidate in 1924.) Other members included John Foster Dulles, Herbert H. Lehman, Henry L. Stimson, Averell Harriman (the Rockefeller family's public relations expert), and Paul M. Warburg and Otto H. Kahn of the law firm Kuhn, Loeb. From its inception, John D. Rockefeller, Jr., was a regular benefactor, He made annual contributions, as well as a large gift of money toward its first headquarters on East 65th Street, along with corporate donors. In 1944, the widow of the Standard Oil executive Harold I. Pratt donated the family's four-story mansion on the corner of 68th Street and Park Avenue for council use, and this became the CFR's new headquarters, known as The Harold Pratt House.

The New York Times described it as a "school for statesmen," where New York City's most prominent bankers, diplomats, and executives could leisurely ruminate over the great issues of the day, and then quietly advise Washington. "In its elegant East 68th Street town house filled with books, tapestries and oil portraits," said the *Times*, "the council holds selective dinners with visiting heads of state and is the host of countless seminars."

Several of John D. Rockefeller's sons joined the council when they came of age. When David joined in 1949, he was the youngest member, a distinction he maintained for fifteen years. From the early 1950s on, the Council's program of speakers, study groups, and publications provided a forum where critical issues were examined and discussed. The CFR publishes *Foreign Affairs* and an annual report containing the membership roster and an account of its financial affairs. The Council also sponsors public events, but as with Bilderberg meetings, its deliberations are secretive and accessible only to membership, including elected leaders, judges, key media figures and academics, and others in positions of public authority.

"Although the CFR is Manhattan based," noted one critical observer, "its reach is coast-to-coast and beyond. The CFR has affiliate entities (dozens of them in fact) in major cities across the country: locally prominent figures in politics, society and academia are invited to "exclusive" membership in CFR affiliates. These entities bring to their forums well-known global figures and conduct policy seminars which promote the New World Order [NWO] propaganda line of the CFR on the local level. A major part of the establishment's drive for NWO is shaping public opinion—this is so that the voting public will accept the internationalist agenda laid forth by the planners behind the scenes. According to one leading CFR member, the planners of the NWO seek a private consensus on major issues. The power brokers 'will seek to educate attentive audiences so that public opinion will come to reflect the private consensus.' "

As in the Bilderberg Group, claim critics of both organizations, these power brokers seek a consensus regarding what approaches to take toward major international issues. After such a consensus is reached, they use their influence to educate local elites, such as those who make up CFR affiliates around the country, toward what is best for the people.

"The true intention of the CFR," asserted Daniel Estulin in *The True Story of the Bilderberg Group*, "can be found within the pages of the very annual reports they so politely hand out to the public each year."

When you examine the CFR's life membership, he stated, you will find most belong to the Bilderberg Group. He and other critics contend that the CFR's real purpose is the promotion of a world government and the elimination of national sovereignty. As evidence, they cite the late Richard Harwood, the former Ombudsman for *The Washington Post*. Calling the CFR, "the nearest thing we have to a ruling establishment in the United States," he wrote in the October 30, 1993, issue of the *Post*, "The president [Bill Clinton] is a member. So is his secretary of state, the deputy secretary of state, all five of the undersecretaries, several of the assistant secretaries and the department's legal adviser. The president's national security adviser and his deputy are members. The director of Central Intelligence (like all previous directors) and the chairman of the Foreign Intelligence Advisory Board are members."

Other CFR members were the secretary of defense, the secretaries of the departments of housing and urban development, interior, health and human services, along with Thomas Foley, speaker of the House, a Bilderberger. On its Internet website, the CFR listed among "Frequently Asked Questions" (FAQ) these queries and answers:

"Why are senior government officials, members of the U.S. Congress, journalists, and corporate executives members of the Council?

"Membership in the Council can represent both the recognition of exceptional achievement in a career involving international affairs, as well as the promise of one. It is important to avoid reversing the causal order in this question. The Council does not 'anoint' government officials, nor advance the careers of those in other fields; it does exert great effort to attract individuals who have displayed significant dedication, expertise, and success in professions concerning American foreign policy and world affairs, and also to encourage them to help in our mission by participating in our meetings and other activities.

"How are individuals selected for membership?

"Every candidate for membership must be a U.S. citizen or a permanent resident with an application for citizenship pending. Candidates are formally proposed in writing by one member and seconded by a minimum of three other individuals. Letters of support from members (as opposed to non-members) are strongly encouraged. Quality, diversity, and balance are the key objectives sought by the Council in the composition of its membership."

The CFR's purpose, said Republican Senator and 1964 presidential candidate Barry Goldwater, was "to destroy the sovereignty of the United States and create a One World Government." In 1979 he declared, "Almost without exception, its members are united by a congeniality of birth, economic status and educational background. They have no ideological anchors. In their pursuit of a New World Order, they are prepared to deal without prejudice with a communist state, a socialist state, a democratic state, a monarchy, an oligarchy. It's all the same to them. Their goal is to impose a benign stability on the quarreling family of nations through merger and consolidation. They see the elimination of national boundaries, the suppression of racial and ethnic loyalties, as the most expeditious avenue to world peace. They believe economic competition is the root cause of international tension."

Discussing the CFR's contention that its vision of the future would reduce wars, lessen poverty and bring about a more efficient utilization of world resources, Goldwater said that "this would inevitably be accompanied by a loss in personal freedom of choice and re-establishment of the restraints that provoked the American revolution." Recalling that since 1945 three different Republicans had occupied the White House for sixteen years, and four Democrats held this most powerful post for seventeen years, and with the exception of the first seven years of the Eisenhower administration, there had been no appreciable change in foreign or domestic policy direction, he pointed out, "There has been a great turnover in personnel, but no change in policy. Example: During the Nixon years, Henry Kissinger, a council member and Nelson Rockefeller protegé, was in charge of foreign policy. When Jimmy Carter was elected, Kissinger was replaced by Zbigniew Brzezinski, a Council member and David Rockefeller protegé."

In 1962, Goldwater noted, Nelson Rockefeller, in a lecture at Harvard University on the interdependence of nations had said that the nation-state, standing alone, threatened in many ways to seem as anachronistic as the Greek city-state eventually became in ancient times. "Everything he said was true," Goldwater said. "We are dependent on other nations for raw materials and for markets. It is necessary to have defense alliances with other nations in order to balance the military power of those who would destroy us. Where I differ from Rockefeller is in the suggestion that to achieve this new federalism, the United States must submerge its national identity and surrender substantial matters of sovereignty to a new political order."

Goldwater noted that in describing the Trilateral commission, "Rockefeller said that he intended to bring the best brains of the world together to bear on the problems of the future." Finding nothing inherently sinister in this original proposal, Goldwater went on, "Examination of the membership roster established beyond question that all those invited to join were members of the power elite, enlisted with skill and singleness of purpose from the banking, commercial, political and communications sectors.

"In my view," Goldwater warned, "the Trilateral Commission represents a skillful, coordinated effort to seize control and consolidate the four centers of power—political, monetary, intellectual and ecclesiastical All this is to be done in the interest of creating a more peaceful, more productive world community. The Trilateral Commission approach is strictly economic. No recognition is given to the political condition. Total reliance is placed on materialism. . . . What it proposes to substitute is an international economy managed and controlled by international monetary groups. No attempt has been made to explain why the people of the Western world enjoy economic abundance. Freedom, spiritual, political, economic, is denied any importance in the Trilateral construction of the next century.

"To accomplish their purpose," said Goldwater, "they mobilized the money power of the Wall Street bankers, the intellectual influence of the academic community . . . and the media controllers represented in the membership of the Council on Foreign Relations and the Trilateral Commission."

Eight years after Goldwater's criticism of the CFR and the Trilateral Commission, Senator Jesse Helms saw "a campaign against the American people, against traditional American culture and values" orchestrated by "a vast array of interests comprising not only the Eastern establishment but also the radical left" that included the Department of State, the Department of Commerce, banks and multinational corporations, the media, the educational establishment, the entertainment industry, and the large tax-exempt foundations "in order to create what some refer to as a New World Order."

Helms named private organizations such as the Council on Foreign Relations, the Trilateral Commission, and Bilderberg that "serve to disseminate and to coordinate the plans for this so-called New World Order in powerful business, financial, academic, and official circles." The viewpoint of what he called "the establishment" was "globalism."

"Not so long ago," he said, "this viewpoint was called the 'one-world' view by its critics. The phrase is no longer fashionable among sophisticates; yet, the phrase 'one-world' is still apt because nothing has changed in the minds and actions of those promoting policies consistent with its fundamental tenets. In the globalist point of view, nation-states and national boundaries do not count for anything. Political philosophies and political principles seem to become simply relative. Indeed, even constitutions are irrelevant to the exercise of power. Liberty and tyranny are viewed as neither necessarily good nor evil, and certainly not a component of policy. . . . All that matters to this club is the maximization of profits resulting from the practice of what can be described as finance capitalism, a system which rests upon the twin pillars of debt and monopoly. This isn't real capitalism. It is the road to economic concentration and to political slavery."

The CFR, wrote Georgetown University professor of history Carroll Quigley in his book *Tragedy and Hope*, "believes national boundaries should be obliterated and one-world rule established." Scholar and author Wilson Blase wrote, "The CFR is the promotional arm of the Ruling Elite in the United States of America. Most influential politicians, academics and media personalities are members, and it uses its influence to infiltrate the New World Order into American life. Its 'experts' write scholarly pieces to be used in decision making, the academics expound on the wisdom of a united world, and the media members disseminate the message."

This openness is a dramatic contrast to the secrecy enveloping the Bilderberg Group. They also differ in the extent of their membership. The CFR has thousands of members. The Bilderberg Group meetings are limited to around one hundred. While they are the same in having a requirement that members not quote one another, the CFR frequently opens its meeting to allow television broadcast of speeches by a president, secretary of state, or other government official. Bilderberg meetings are closed to the press. Both groups publish their membership lists. While the CFR has a website, the Bilderberg Group does not. Telephone inquiries for CFR information are welcomed. Those to Bilderberg offices in the Netherlands and New York are not.

While the CFR's ancestry is found in the aftermath of World War I, and Dr. Joseph Retinger fathered Bilderberg after World War II, the parenthood in 1973 of their even more controversial younger brother, the Trilateral Commission, was proudly claimed by David Rockefeller. "No organization with which I have played a founding role," he wrote, "has attracted as much public scrutiny as the Trilateral Commission."

Inspiration for the Trilateral Commission was found in Zbigniew Brzezinski's 1970 book *Between Two Ages*. Published while he was a professor at Columbia University, it was read by Rockefeller, who found its argument for linking North America, Western Europe, and Japan in their economic, political, and defense relations compelling. The idea coincided with Rockefeller's realization that power relationships in the world had fundamentally changed. Although still dominant, the United States had declined relatively in terms of its economic power as both Western Europe and Japan recovered from World War II and entered a period of dramatic economic growth and expansion. "As a result the comity that characterized relationships among these regions for more than two decades had deteriorated alarmingly," Rockefeller wrote, "and I believed something needed to be done."

He spoke about this in March 1972 before Chase International Financial Forums in Montreal, London, Brussels, and Paris, calling for an "international commission for peace and prosperity," that would be composed of private citizens drawn from the NATO countries and Japan in order to examine "such vital fields as international trade and investment; environmental problems; control of crime and drugs; population control; and assistance to developing nations."

Having read Brzezinski's book, Rockefeller boarded a flight to Belgium for the 1972 meeting of the Bilderberg Group, to which Brzezinski had been invited.

"I had been urging the Steering Committee to invite Japanese participants for several years," Rockefeller recalled, "and at our session that April, I was again politely but firmly told no. Zbig [Zbigniew] considered this rebuff further proof that my idea was well founded and urged me to pursue it. I arranged a follow-up meeting with Zbig, Robert Bowie of the Center for International Studies at Harvard, Henry Owen of the Brookings Institution, and McGeorge Bundy of the Ford Foundation, who all heartily endorsed my proposal to form a trilateral organization."

Rockefeller convened a group that included five Europeans and four Japanese for a meeting at his country home in the summer of 1972. Following a lengthy discussion, they agreed to set up the new organization. Brzezinski was named director.

"Trilateral was established on a trial basis," Rockefeller wrote. "At the end of three years we would review its activities and accomplishments and decide whether it should be continued. Each region had its own executive committee and secretariat. At our first executive committee meeting in Tokyo in October 1973, two task forces reported on political and monetary relations among the three regions, and we published their findings in an effort to influence the behavior of our respective governments. For the second executive committee meeting in Brussels in June 1974, just after the first OPEC 'oil shock' and calls for a 'new international economic order,' we concentrated on the energy crisis and relations with developing countries."

Stating that they cast their nets widely in terms of membership, Rockefeller recorded that they recruited labor union leaders, corporate chief executives, prominent Democrats and Republicans, as well as distinguished academics, university presidents, and the heads of not-for-profits involved overseas. They assembled what he believed were "the best minds in America," with Europeans and Japanese delegations "of comparable distinction."

The inclusion among the first group of an obscure Democratic governor of Georgia, James Earl Carter, Rockefeller noted, had an unintended consequence. A week after the first Trilateral executive committee meeting in Washington, DC, in December 1975, Carter announced that he would seek the Democratic nomination for president of the United States. Critical Bilderberg watchers would note that Carter had attended a Bilderberg meeting and had been marked by the Group for ascendancy.

Funding for the Trilateral Commission came from Rockefeller, the Charles Kettering Foundation, and the Ford Foundation. Because of cross-membership, the Trilaterals appeared to be an inner circle of the Council on Foreign Relations, with ties to the Atlantic Institute for International Affairs, which was established in 1961.

"A Trilateral Commission Task Force Report, presented during the 1975 meeting in Kyoto, Japan, called *An Outline for Remaking World Trade and Finance*, said, 'Close Trilateral cooperation in keeping the peace, in managing the world economy, and in fostering economic development and in alleviating world poverty, will improve the chances of a smooth and peaceful evolution of the global system.' "

Another Commission document read, "The overriding goal is to make the world safe for interdependence by protecting the benefits which it provides for each country against external and internal threats which will constantly emerge from those willing to pay a price for more national autonomy. This may sometimes require slowing the pace at which interdependence proceeds, and checking some aspects of it. More frequently however, it will call for checking the intrusion of national government into the international exchange of both economic and non-economic goods."

The Trilateral Commission's "organizational structure consisted of a ten-member Executive Committee, made up of a regional chairman, a deputy chairman, and a director for each of the three areas. Rockefeller was the chairman for the North American sector. An eleven member American Executive Committee nominated candidates for its delegation, based on their profession, their involvement in international affairs and taking into account their place of residence, so they could have a geographical balance. . . . The Commission holds an annual three-day meeting, rotated among the three areas, to talk about the world monetary situation, and other economic and military issues. Following the Bilderberg policy, meetings are closed to the public, and the media is denied access."

Envisioned as lasting only three years, the Trilateral Commission has been renewed for successive three-year periods (triennia). "When the first was launched in 1973, states the Commission's official history, the immediate purpose was "to draw together—at a time of considerable friction among governments—the highest level unofficial group possible to look together at the key common problems facing our three areas." "At a deeper level, there was a sense that the United States was no longer in such a singular leadership position as it had been in earlier post–World War II years, and that a more shared form of leadership, including Europe and Japan in particular, would be needed for the international system to navigate successfully the major challenges of the coming years." The organization had published a quarterly magazine, called the *Trialogue.* The first three issues of the year were devoted to significant international matters, while the fourth, covered in detail, their annual meeting. It was discontinued in 1985 to help lower expenses. Trilateral Commission *Task Force Reports* usually take up to a year to prepare, and they are always written by at least three experts, representing each region. The Commission has had some of its members in such branches of the media as *The New York Times, The Washington Post, The Wall Street Journal, Minneapolis Star and Tribune, Los Angeles Times, Chicago Sun-Times, Kyodo News Service, Japan Times, La Stampa, Die Ziet, The Financial Times, The Economist, Time* magazine, Japan Broadcasting Corporation, CBS, and the Associated Press. An official history of the Commission asserted that it "remains as important as ever in helping our countries fulfill their shared leadership responsibilities in the wider international system and [that] its framework needs to be widened to reflect broader changes in the world. . . . The 'growing interdependence' that so impressed the founders of the Trilateral Commission in the early 1970s is deepening into 'globalization.' "

The history continued, "The need for shared thinking and leadership by the Trilateral countries, who (along with the principal international organizations) remain the primary anchors of the wider international system, has not diminished but, if anything, intensified. At the same time, their leadership must change to take into account the dramatic transformation of the international system. As relations with other countries become more mature—and power more diffuse—the leadership tasks of the original Trilateral countries need to be carried out with others to an increasing extent."

The membership of the "Trilateral Commission consists of about 350 leaders in business, news media, academia, public service . . . labor unions, and other non-governmental organizations from the three regions. The regional chairmen, deputy chairmen, and directors constitute leadership of the Trilateral Commission, along with an Executive Committee including about forty other members. The annual meeting of Commission members rotates among the three regions. It was held in Washington in 2008 and Brussels in 2007. The 2009 was scheduled for Tokyo." The work of the "Commission generally involved teams of authors from the three regions working together for a year or more on draft reports which were discussed in draft form in the annual meeting and then published" as Triangle Papers.

"The regional groups within the Trilateral Commission carry on some activities of their own. The European Group, with its secretariat based in Paris, holds an annual weekend meeting each fall. The North American Group, with its secretariat based in Washington, DC, began North American regional meetings in 2002 and occasionally gathered with a special speaker for a dinner or luncheon event. The Pacific Asian Group, with secretariat based in Tokyo, began regional meetings in 2000. Each region carried on its own fund-raising to provide the financial support needed for the Trilateral Commission's work."

In a letter to the editor of *The Washington Post*, David Rockefeller said, "I have never ceased to be amazed at those few among us who spot a conspiracy under every rock, a cabal in every corner. . . . To some, the Trilateral Commission is a sinister plot by Eastern Establishment businessmen who will do almost anything—including going into cahoots with the Kremlin—for the sake of financial gain. . . . As founder of the Trilateral Commission and its current North American chairman, I am usually singled out as the 'cabalist-in-chief.' One recent tirade had me orchestrating a plot 'to reduce New York's population to approximately four million and siphon off the surplus population into slave labor camps.' The same publication asserts that I'm already responsible for a fascist scheme in Latin America that 'led to shifts in global weather patterns, marked by droughts and severe winters in the United States.'"

Stating that "the reality is much less juicy than the theories," Rockefeller wrote, "The Trilateral Commission now has about 300 members from North America, Western Europe and Japan. About one quarter are from the United States and include not only business people but labor union leaders, university professors and research institute directors, congressmen and senators, media representatives and others. There are about as many Republicans and Democrats, and most regions of the nation are represented.

"The Trilateral Commission does not take positions on issues or endorse individuals for elective or appointive office," said Rockefeller. As to whether it was secretive, he wrote, "Not at all. For $10 a year, anyone can subscribe to its quarterly magazine, *Trialogue*, and also receive periodic mailings of task force reports. The only part of the proceedings that were off the record," he said, "were discussions at commission meetings" that were kept private "to encourage uninhibited criticism and debate.

"Far from being a coterie of international conspirators with designs on covertly conquering the world," he asserted that "the Trilateral Commission is, in reality, a group of concerned citizens interested in identifying and clarifying problems facing the world and in fostering greater understanding of cooperation among international allies."

Every president's administration since Carter has had top-level Trilateral Commission representation through the president or vice president or both. Serving as secretary of state were Henry Kissinger (Nixon, Ford), Cyrus Vance (Carter), Alexander Haig and George Shultz (Reagan), Lawrence Eagleburger (G. H. W. Bush), Warren Christopher (Clinton), and Madeleine Albright (Clinton). Acting secretaries of state included Philip Habib (Carter), Michael Armacost (G. H. W. Bush), Arnold Kantor (Clinton), and Richard Cooper (Clinton).

Since the founding of the Trilateral Commission in 1973, there have been only seven World Bank presidents. Six were members of the Trilateral Commission: Robert McNamara (1968–81), A. W. Clausen (1981–86), Barber Conable (1986–1991), Lewis Preston (1991–1995), James Wolfensohn (1995–2005), Paul Wolfowitz (2005–2007), Robert Zoellick (2007). In the position of U.S. Trade Representative (USTR) since 1977, eight of ten have been members of the Trilateral

Commission: Robert S. Strauss (1977–1979), Reubin O'D. Askew (1979–1981), William E. Brock III (1981–1985), Clayton K. Yeutter (1985–1989), Carla A. Hills (1989–1993), Mickey Kantor (1993–1997), Charlene Barshefsky (1997–2001), Robert Zoellick (2001–2005), Rob Portman (2005–2006), and Susan Schwab (2006). The Federal Reserve Board has also had Trilaterals as chairman: Arthur Burns (1970–1978), Paul Volcker (1979–1987), and Alan Greenspan (1987–2006).

Having been chosen by David Rockefeller to serve as first director of the Trilateral Commission in 1973, Brzezinski became President Carter's national security advisor. Replacing Henry Kissinger, he emphasized further development of the U.S.-China relationship, favored a new arms control agreement with Moscow, and shared the president and Secretary of State Cyrus Vance's view that the United States should seek international cooperation in its diplomacy instead of going it alone.

Out of government during the Reagan and Clinton administrations, Brzezinski was back in public prominence in the 2008 presidential election campaign as national security advisor to Senator Barack Obama. Noting he had been a member of the Bilderberg Group, the Trilateral Commission, and the CFR, perennial New World Order alarmists, such as Jim Tucker and Alex Jones, along with Internet bloggers, claimed that Obama also had political and financial backing of other Bilderberg, CFR, and Trilateral members, and that his wife, Michelle, was associated with the Chicago CFR.

In a CNN broadcast on March 31, 2008, Obama was reported to have told a campaign rally in Lancaster, Pennsylvania, that worries about One World Order and a North American Union had been "ginned up by the blogs and the Internet." Responding to a question from the audience, asking whether he was a member of CFR, he replied, "I don't know if I'm an official member. I've spoken there before. It basically is a forum where people talk about foreign policy. There is no official membership. I don't have a card, or you know a special handshake or anything like that." The report noted that Senator Hillary Clinton had spoken several times to the CFR, but it noted that often because the council served as lightning rod for conspiracy theorists, candidates shied away from listing their affiliation with the group. For example, the report said that Vice President Cheney was a former director but had taken pains not to publicize the fact. He told a meeting of the CFR in a speech broadcast on C-SPAN, "I've been a member for long and was actually a director for some period of time. I never mentioned that when I was running for re-election back home in Wyoming."

Obama dismissed notions that the council had been at the center of several One World Order conspiracies with theorists contending that the group conspired to bring about one world government and a North American Union similar to the EU. "I see no evidence of this actually taking place," he said.

Ominously on March 23, 2008, PrisonPlanet columnist Paul Joseph Watson wrote, "It has been announced that Bilderberg luminary and top corporate elitist James A. Johnson will select Democratic candidate Barack Obama's running mate for the 2008 election and in turn potentially act as kingmaker for America's future president." Watson noted that Johnson also selected John Kerry's running mate, John Edwards, in 2004 after Edwards had "impressed Bilderberg elitists Henry Kissinger and David Rockefeller with a speech he gave at the globalist confab in Italy that year." Watson added, "The news further puts to rest any delusions that Bilderberg is a mere talking shop where no decisions are made." Reporting that Johnson was said to be a member of "American Friends of Bilderberg," an offshoot of the Bilderberg Group that accepted donations to fund Bilderberg meetings, Watson wrote that Johnson attended Bilderberg meetings and, therefore, "can be classed as a Bilderberg luminary. . . . Predictably," said Watson, "he is also a member of the Trilateral Commission and the Council on Foreign Relations."

At the end of his discussion of Bilderberg, the CFR, and the Trilateral Commission in his memoirs, David Rockefeller concluded, "The world has now become so inextricably intertwined that the United States can no longer go it alone, as some prominent politicians have urged that we should do. We are the world's sole superpower and its dominant nation economically. One of our principal duties is to provide judicious and consistent leadership that is firmly embedded in our national values and ideals. To do otherwise is to guarantee our return to the conflict that characterized the blood-drenched twentieth century. It is that fear, and that hope, that makes me a proud internationalist."

• Fifteen •

THE NORTH AMERICAN UNION

The Almighty Dollar. The Greenback. The Buck. Following World War I, there was nowhere in the world that anyone was likely to turn down an opportunity to pocket American currency. Replacing the British pound sterling and the French and Swiss franc, it became the universal means of exchange. Even when the United States went off the gold standard, the dollar remained the backbone of international commerce. A prediction that the day might come when the dollar would go the way of the coins of Ancient Rome and the Spanish doubloon would have been greeted with derision. Yet, the disappearance of the U.S. dollar is said to be the inevitable result of the globalization that is being promoted by the Bilderbergers and other internationalists.

The demise of the dollar would be the consequence of the formation of the "North American Union," that in turn would become an amalgamation of all the countries of the Western Hemisphere into a United States of the Americas, followed by a world government.

As the EU adopted the Euro, the North American Union would have as its currency the "Amero."

According to those who foresee these events, and vehemently warn against them, the first step toward a North American Union was NAFTA. This was followed by a conference at Baylor University in Waco, Texas, on March 23, 2005, between President George W. Bush,

Canadian prime minister Paul Martin, and Mexican president Vicente Fox. They announced an "initiative" that they called the "Security and Prosperity Partnership of North America" (SPP). They said it was designed to "establish a common continental security perimeter against outside threats while facilitating the legal flow of people and trade across shared borders and increasing cooperation on energy, the environment and bioterrorism."

"Among other things," reported Peter Baker in *The Washington Post*, "the three governments agreed to develop standardized rules for the screening of people and cargo arriving in North America, regardless of which country is the first point of entry. They noted that with the three countries bound together by the North American Free Trade Agreement of 1994, nearly a third of U.S. trade is conducted with Canada and Mexico, with the thousands of miles of borders the United States shares with the two countries expected to be crossed nearly 400 million times in 2005."

"We've got a large border with Canada; we've got a large border with Mexico," said President Bush. "There are some million people a day crossing the border from Mexico to the United States, which presents a common issue, and that is: how do we make sure those crossing the border are not terrorists or drug runners or gun runners or smugglers?"

"Against the backdrop of these security concerns, the three leaders said they wanted to build on NAFTA and enhance economic integration to better compete against competitors such as the European Union, China and India."

On April 27, 2007, the ministers of the three countries responsible for transportation in North America met in Tucson, Arizona, in order to confirm and advance the three nations' commitment to developing coordinated, compatible, and interconnected national systems of transportation. In a joint statement, they said, "We affirm that such systems will support our shared vision for increased economic and social development, trade, tourism, cooperation and a healthy environment among our countries in the 21st century. We have met for the first time in Tucson to consider the future of our shared transporation interests in an increasingly globalized world."

During the discussions, they highlighted the fact that the globalization of economies had yielded strong economic benefits but that it had also put pressure on ports, borders and airports. They recognized that because many of the most important infrastructure facilities are located in urban areas, "greater volumes of international freight and passenger traffic, when combined with increasing local traffic, and without offsetting policies and programs, will result in greater congestion, delay, degradation of environmental quality and higher shipping and travel costs." Citing "real economic benefits in North America" resulting from "open and fair trade, transparency in economic regulations, and sound, market-based economic policies," they said that actions "to facilitate commerce across our borders in all modes of transport, especially in road transport, will improve supply chain and logistics processes and provide for continued North American competitiveness."

Phyllis Schlafly, a leading opponent of proposals for North American integration, wrote on July 13, 2005, "The Council on Foreign Relations (CFR) has just let the cat out of the bag about what's really behind our trade agreements and security partnerships with the other North American countries. A 59-page CFR document spells out a five-year plan for the 'establishment by 2010 of a North American economic and security community' with a common 'outer security perimeter.' "

She warned that "community" meant "integrating the United States with corruption, socialism, poverty and the population of Mexico and Canada," and that "common perimeter meant wide-open U.S. borders between the U.S., Mexico and Canada. The CFR document laid the groundwork for the freer flow of people within North America. Common security perimeter would require the United States to harmonize visa and asylum regulations with Mexico and Canada, harmonize entry screening, and fully share data about the exit and entry of foreign nationals." It called for creating a "North American preference so that employers can recruit low-paid workers from anywhere in North America. No longer will illegal aliens have to be smuggled across the border; employers can openly recruit foreigners willing to work for a fraction of U.S. wages.

"The document's frequent references to security," Schlafly continued, "are just a cover for the real objectives. The document's 'security cooperation' includes the registration of ballistics and explosives, while Canada specifically refused to cooperate with our Strategic Defense Initiative (SDI). To no one's surprise, the CFR plan calls for massive U.S. foreign aid to the other countries. The burden on the U.S. taxpayers will include so-called 'multilateral development' from the World Bank and the Inter-American Development Bank, 'long-term loans in pesos,' and a North American Investment Fund to send U.S. private capital to Mexico."

She asserted that "the experience of the European Union and the World Trade Organization made it clear that a common market required a court system," and noted that the "CFR document called for a permanent tribunal for North American dispute resolution. Get ready for decisions from non-American judges who make up their rules ad hoc," she wrote, "and probably hate the United States anyway."

During the Waco meeting, the two presidents and prime minister said they saw "a need for adequate transportation infrastructure and efficient transportation services within and between" the U.S., Mexico, and Canada. A central feature of this would be a ten-lane, 400-yard-wide superhighway from the Mexican port of Lázaro Cárdenas, up to and across the U.S. border, all the way to Canada. Within the median strip dividing the north and south car and truck lanes would be railway lines and oil and gas pipelines.

In 2006, Texas Republican congressman (and 2008 presidential candidate) Ron Paul wrote, "Governor Rick Perry [a Bilderberg attendee] is a supporter of the superhighway project, and Congress has provided small amounts of money to study the proposal. Since this money was just one item in an enormous transportation appropriations bill, however, most members of Congress were not aware of it. The proposed highway is part of a broader plan advanced by a quasi-government organization called the 'Security and Prosperity Partnership of North America,' or SPP."

Noting that the SPP was first launched in 2005 by the heads of state of the United States, Canada, and Mexico, at the summit in Waco, Texas, Paul said that it was not created by a treaty between the nations involved, nor was Congress involved in any way. He said SPP "is an unholy alliance of foreign consortiums and officials from several governments," and he asserted that it "is not the result of free market demand, but rather an extension of government-managed trade schemes like NAFTA that benefit politically connected interests."

The real issue, said the maverick and feisty congressman, is national sovereignty. "Once again," he complained, "decisions that affect millions of Americans are not being made by those Americans themselves, or even by their elected representatives in Congress. Instead, a handful of elites use their government connections to bypass national legislatures and ignore our Constitution, which expressly grants Congress sole authority to regulate international trade. The ultimate goal is not simply a superhighway but an integrated North American Union—complete with a currency, a cross-national bureaucracy, and virtually borderless travel within the Union. Like the European Union, a North American Union would represent another step toward the abolition of national sovereignty altogether."

After Paul participated in a Republican presidential-candidates' debate, a dubious article by *Los Angeles Times* staff writer Stephen Braun on November 30, 2007, noted that "Paul's followers talk about such conspiracy theories as 'merging the United States with Canada and Mexico'," and that the "Texas congressman coolly raised the specter of a dire new national threat—an as-yet unbuilt superhighway."

Observing that federal and state highway and trade officials and their transportation consultants reacted with "befuddlement and amusement," the article cited denials by federal officials. "The fearsome secret international highway project Paul described," they said, "does not exist." Ian Grossman, a spokesman with the Federal Highway Administration, said, "There is no such superhighway like the one he's talking about. It doesn't exist, in plans or anywhere else."

"It's complete fiction," said Tiffany Melvin, the executive director of NASCO, a consortium of transportation agencies and business interests caught in what Braun called "the crosshairs of anti-highway activists. This is the work of fringe groups that have wrapped a couple of separate projects together into one big paranoid fantasy."

A "loose confederation of conservative Internet bloggers and some right-wing groups, among them the John Birch Society," Braun wrote, "has seized on a burst of activity in federal highway projects in recent years as evidence that the Bush administration is pushing toward a European Union-style government for North America."

"The problem," said public officials, "was that the new emphasis on highway construction reflects a growing concern about renewing a crumbling U.S. road system, not a secret extension of the North American Free Trade Agreement."

"These whispers have been around in some form or another ever since NAFTA was signed," said Grossman, who pointed out that numerous U.S. highways already are connected to Mexican and Canadian thoroughfares.

Braun noted that "Paul had taken up the issue in recent years, sounding alarms in the Congressional Record after activists rallied against a $1 billion Texas project that aimed to build a privately financed highway corridor from the border with Mexico to the Oklahoma state line."

The article said that Paul "also linked the purported NAFTA highway to his concerns about the Trilateral Commission, an enduring bugaboo of conspiracy theorists—and the World Trade Organization's control of our drug industry and our nutritional products."

"I don't like big government in Washington," Paul said, "so I don't like this trend toward international government."

"The anti-highway movement," Braun explained to *Los Angeles Times* readers, "had surged from a Texas-based group, CorridorWatch.org, to old-line groups like the Birch Society and to Jerome Corsi, a conservative author who aided the Swift boat targeting of Sen. John F. Kerry during the 2004 campaign," and would publish *Obama Nation* in 2008. "As the alarms about NAFTA's illusory highway have spread across the Web, the issues of paranoia had ignited sparks of humor. Comedy Central's mock commentator Stephen Colbert took up the issue, saying the highway plan was real 'because I got it from the Internet.' He added that 'it's a plan to make Canada, the U.S. and Mexico one country and force us to eat moose tacos.' "

Finding nothing amusing in the alleged highway project, former independent presidential candidate, columnist, and commentator Pat Buchanan called it the "NAFTA Super Highway" and claimed that the cost beyond the dollars needed to build it would be the demise of the "once independent American republic." He cited testimony by Dr. Robert Pastor, vice chair of the CFR Task Force on North America before a panel of the Senate Committee on Foreign Relations, in which Pastor called "for erasing all U.S. borders and the merger of the United States, Mexico and Canada in a North American union stretching from Prudhoe Bay to Guatemala."

"What we need to do," Pastor reportedly asserted, "is forge a new North American Community. Instead of stopping North Americans on the borders, we ought to provide them with a secure, biometric Border Pass that would ease transit across the border like an E-Z pass permits our cars to speed through tolls."

Buchanan wrote, "Under the Pastor-CFR plan, the illegal alien invasion would be solved by eliminating America's borders and legalizing the invasion. We would no longer defend the Rio Grande."

To achieve economic integration of what Buchanan called "Mexamerica," north–south highways and railways would be built "to weld the United States, Canada and Mexico together" as the American Union was welded by the Northern Pacific, Union Pacific, and Southern Pacific and by the interstate highway system begun during the Eisenhower administration.

Speaking in Madrid, Spain, in 2002, noted Buchanan, Mexican president Vicente Fox declared that the "long-range objective is to establish with the United States . . . an ensemble of connections and institutions similar to those created by the European Union," with the goal of freedom of movement of capital, goods, services, and persons.

"The new framework we wish to construct," Fox reportedly said, "is inspired in the example of the European Union."

The critical element of the Fox post-NAFTA agenda, Buchanan stated, was "absolute freedom of movement for persons between Mexico and the United States" to bring about "a merger" and "complete integration" of the two nations.

"When Fox proposed his merger of America and Mexico in a North American Union," wrote Buchanan, "Robert Bartley, for thirty years editorial page editor of *The Wall Street Journal*, declared him a 'visionary' and pledged solidarity."

Declaring that the American people never supported NAFTA, and they are angry over [President George W.] Bush's failure to secure the border—but a shotgun marriage between our two nations appears prearranged."

Describing the highway as "this Fox-Bush autobahn," Buchanan continued, "container ships from China would unload at Lázaro Cárdenas, a port named for the Mexican president who nationalized all U.S. oil companies in 1938. From there, trucks with Mexican drivers would run fast lines into the United States, hauling their cargo to a U.S. customs inspection terminal, in Kansas City, Missouri. From there, the trucks would fan out across America or roll on into Canada. Similar superhighways from Mexico through the United States into Canada are planned. The beneficiaries of this NAFTA Super Highway project would be the contractors who build it and the importers and outlet stores for the Chinese-manufactured goods that would come flooding in. The losers would be U.S. longshoremen, truckers, manufacturers and taxpayers."

Others who feel they should sound an alarm over the "NAFTA Super Highway project" suggest that another step in creating a "United States of North America" was taken with the adoption of the Free and Secure Trade (FAST) program. It is described as the "border accord initiative" between the United States, Mexico, and Canada designed to ensure security and safety while enhancing the economic prosperity of each country." In developing this program, Mexico, Canada, and the United States have agreed to coordinate, to the maximum extent possible, their commercial processes for clearance of commercial shipments at the border. FAST promotes "free and secure trade by using common risk-management principles, supply chain security, industry partnership, and advanced technology to improve the efficiency of screening and clearing commercial traffic at our shared borders."

"Eligibility for the FAST program requires participants (carrier, drivers, and importers) to submit an application and an agreement, along with a security profile, depending on their role in the Customs and Trade Partnership Against Terrorism (C-TPAT) and FAST programs. The FAST program allows known low-risk participants to receive expedited border processing. This enables U.S. Customs and Border Protection (CBP) to redirect security efforts and inspections where needed most—on commerce that is high risk, or unknown risk—while ensuring easy movement of legitimate, low-risk commerce." Much of the suspicion surrounding NAFTA, a trans-United States superhighway, and a conspiracy to create a United States of North America, with the "Amero" replacing the dollar, is fueled by the Internet and the freewheeling opinion-expressing known as the "Blogosphere." As one posting noted, "To be fair, harboring some degree of unrest pertaining to the agreement is not unfounded." It pointed out that NAFTA was originally conceived by George H. W. Bush as an expansion to the Canada-U.S. Free Trade Agreement of 1988. It passed through Congress in 1993 under the Clinton administration by a vote of 61–38. Technically and theoretically, it is a legally binding agreement between Mexico, Canada, and the United States, but not a treaty, which the Constitution requires the Senate to approve with a two-thirds vote. Because NAFTA was an agreement, it only required a simple majority to be ratified.

Since its adoption, NAFTA has been blamed for contributing to deindustrialization of the United States through outsourcing of jobs to Mexico. Among those faulting NAFTA were 2008 Democratic presidential candidates Barack Obama and Hillary Clinton, although her husband supported it.

As to allegations about the superhighway stretching between Mexico and Canada, *Seattle Times* columnist Phillip Dine quoted David Bohigian, U.S. assistant secretary of commerce, as stating that "there is absolutely no U.S. government plan for a NAFTA superhighway of any sort."

To put this "conspiracy" in perspective, there are just over 1,000,000 Google "hits" for a World Trade Center attacks conspiracy, when "North American Union" yields more than sixty times that number.

The "conspiracy" issue can get personal. Cliff Kincaid, editor of the *Accuracy in Media* (AIM) *Report* challenged Democratic Party foreign policy specialist Robert Pastor, a former official of the Carter administration and director of the Center for North American Studies at American University (CNAS) for having claimed that a " 'very small group' of Conservatives was unfairly accusing him of being at the center of a 'vast conspiracy' to implement the idea of a North American Union by 'stealth.' " Calling the charges "absurd," Pastor spoke at a conference devoted to the development of a North American legal system.

One panel of the conference (similar to the Bilderberg Group meetings) was devoted to analyzing how NAFTA could be expanded into the areas of intellectual property and taxation and regulations. Stephen Zamora of the University of Houston Law School, reportedly attacked the idea of a wall separating Mexico and the United States, in order to control illegal immigration, asking, "What does citizenship mean anymore?"

Another speaker, Tom Farer, dean of the Graduate School of International Studies at the University of Denver, was said to have made a point of stating that his own congressman, Tom Tancredo, a Colorado Republican and advocate of U.S. border security, was a backward thinker. According to Kincaid, the luncheon speaker at the conference was "Eric Farnsworth, the vice president of the Council of the Americas." Its honorary chairman is Bilderberg Group co-founder David Rockefeller, and "one of the key board members is Thomas F. McLarty III, president of Henry Kissinger's international consulting firm Kissinger McLarty Associates," formed with McLarty, "who had served as Bill Clinton's White House counselor and chief of staff when NAFTA was signed and passed by Congress."

One of the rare instances of a discussion of the NAFTA superhighway and mention of the Bilderberg Group on television occurred on Fox News Channel's *Special Report with Brit Hume* and his panel of "all stars," consisting of Juan Williams of National Public Radio; Fred Barnes of *The Weekly Standard*; and syndicated columnist Charles Krauthammer. The discussion went this way:

HUME: Well, the politicians laugh it off, and if you ask anybody in a position of authority in Washington about the idea that there is a plan well underway to create a North American Union along the lines of the European Union, which would be composed, among other things, of a great big superhighway system that would connect all three countries.

It is a fairly widely believed theory, believe it or not, particularly on the American right, that President Bush and the leaders of the foreign policy establishment want to see these three countries, the United States, Canada, and Mexico, joined and governed, ultimately, by a super government that would be able to overrule the sovereign governments of each of those countries in certain key matters related to trade, and who knows what else. The literature on it is fairly extensive. But is there any truth to it? Charles?

KRAUTHAMMER: I love this stuff, because if you ever doubt your own sanity, all you have to do is read this stuff and you know that you are okay. Part of this great conspiracy is recent evidence that the governor of Texas, who is a Republican, who supports this highway from Laredo into Oklahoma, was recently at the Bilderberg conference, which is, supposedly, one of these trilateral conferences involving financiers who want to globalize the world and pull strings. But let me tell you—I have spoken to the Bilderberg conference, as has George Will and Paul Gigot, and I can assure you that Gigot and Will and I are not three amigos who are going to order in black helicopters to force Americans to watch hockey on Monday night and soccer on Sundays. The reason the Bilderberg Conference is secret is because its proceedings are so dull that if the transcripts were ever published, nobody would ever attend. What's happening here is that the president organized a meeting a few years ago with the leaders of Mexico and Canada to work out stuff like how to regulate the borders in terms of terrorism, or pandemics, or how much pesticide you can have on a cabbage. This is the piddling stuff that these committees are involved in, and anybody who believes it is about a great North American Union is in the league of people who believe that Elvis is still alive.

WILLIAMS: Well, there are a lot of those.

HUME: Juan, what do you think of this?

WILLIAMS: Elvis is alive, I think that.

HUME: Come on, help me out here.

WILLIAMS: No, it seems to me that it is in our interest to work with our neighbors. No question. And I think we should be doing more work with our neighbors in terms of protecting our borders if you're concerned about terrorism.

HUME: You get around town, and do you hear anybody proposing this idea?

WILLIAMS: No. In fact, as Charles was saying, there is some reality to the highway from Mexico going up through Texas into Oklahoma. But there is no reality, there is just no reality to it yet.

HUME: Fred?

BARNES: Of course Charles would deny having been to a Bilderberg event, but there was nothing going on there. But they always deny it, right? Brit, the only person that I have heard about this North American Union from so far is you and Bret Baer [a Fox News White House correspondent]. How did Bret Baer not break into laughter when he was asking that?

HUME: He was trying to keep a straight face.

BARNES: This charade has been in American politics for years and years. It used to be fear of one world government—our sovereignty was going to be handed over to a one world government. Then the UN turned out to be so pathetic that nobody would believe that. So now they've got the new bogeyman as this North American Union. It is not going to happen. That is ludicrous. There is a particular reason for the origin of the European Union. Those were countries that were fighting wars against each other. And one of the reasons to have the EU was to have peace.

In an article titled "The Amero Conspiracy" in *The Boston Globe*, November 25, 2007, Frank Bennett wrote that in the fall of 2006, author Phyllis Schlafly, along with the conservative author Jerome Corsi and Howard Phillips, founder of the Conservative Caucus, started a Website dedicated to "quashing the coming North American 'Socialist mega-state.' "

On the subject of the creation of a North American Union, Corsi published a best-selling book, *The Late Great U.S.A.* It was this, and columns on the Conservative websites WorldNetDaily and Human Events, that placed him in the fore of those who attribute NAU, NAFTA, and the Amero to a vast globalist conspiracy. Corsi contends that the new North American government will grow out of the national working groups set up by the SPP, with bureaucratic agencies outranking the three national legislatures. A North American Court will be able to overrule national courts. He also predicts the institution of North American passports, and a meshing of the militaries of the U.S., Canada, and Mexico.

"Corsi's warning cry and gift for detail," wrote Bennett in the *Boston Globe*. "have given the theory traction in circles where anxieties about immigration and corporate oligarchy intersect. Lou Dobbs, whose CNN show portrays both free trade and increased immigration as sops to multinational corporations and body blows to the middle class, has devoted investigative segments to the NAU, the Amero, and the

NAFTA Superhighway. The John Birch Society a month ago devoted an entire issue of its magazine to the NAU."

A Bilderberger who spoke on the guarantee of anonymity said that those who see the Group, other internationalist organizations, free-trade advocates, and the CPP as all part of a conspiracy to impose a North American Union as a step to world government are "crazy."

· Sixteen ·

CONSPIRACY OR OLD BOY NETWORK?

In his 1993 biography, *A Life in Progress*, Conrad Black had this to say about "the old boy network" aspect of Bilderberg meetings:

"The key to [their] unique success has been to hold them in remote places almost entirely without spouses or aides, to discourage prepared texts, and to confine discussion as much as possible to English. Although I had first met Henry Kissinger in Palm Beach in 1979, and then at a luncheon in Toronto, jointly hosted by *The Economist* magazine and our company in 1980, and later socially in New York, it was at Bilderberg that I got to know him and a number of our other, future, directors and advisory board members. These included Giovanni Agnelli of Fiat, Dwayne Andreas [controlling shareholder of the giant agribusiness Archer-Daniels, Midland], Zbigniew Brzezinski [former national security advisor in the Carter administration], Lord Carrington [former British foreign and defense secretary and secretary-general of NATO], Andrew Knight [editor of *The Economist*], Richard Perle [former U.S. assistant secretary of National Defense and one of the champions of the Strategic Defense Initiative ("Star Wars") and Euro-missile deployment], Paul Volcker [former Federal Reserve chairman], and George Will [U.S. conservative columnist and commentator], as well as many other interesting people.

"Not having very satisfactory recollections of schooldays, nor being a very enthusiastic or observant university alumnus, Bilderberg has been the closest I have known to that sort of camaraderie. The animated social sessions, as much as the cut and thrust on the principal strategic and economic issues faced by the Atlantic community, have given me, and many other regular participants, a powerful and entirely agreeable sense of community with some very talented and prominent people."

When David Rockefeller discussed Bilderberg in *Memoirs*, published in 2002, he said that he was surprised to have been "one of eleven Americans invited, along with some fifty delegates from eleven Western countries, to the first meeting in 1954. He found he was part of—a lively mosaic of politicians, businessmen, journalists, and trade unionists." Asked to prepare a background paper on prospects for the world economy from the American point of view, he predicted steady economic growth in the United States that contrasted with a "dreary and dismal future" envisioned by former British Labour Party chancellor of the exchequer, Hugh Gaitskell. Stating that his contribution to the first meeting "undoubtedly helped establish my credibility with a sophisticated group of senior politicians and business leaders," he wrote. "For the first twenty years Bilderberg meetings were marked by the sharp clash of opposing views."

Scoffing at "the conspiracy theorists" who have "apocalyptic visions of omnipotent international bankers plotting with unscrupulous government officials to impose cunning schemes on an ignorant and unsuspecting world," he wrote that it is merely "an intensely interesting annual discussion group that debates issues of significance to both Europeans and North Americans" without reaching consensus.

As described by Rockefeller, the Bilderberg Group is as benign as other fraternal organizations and is no more menacing than the Rotary, Kiwanis, the Knights of Columbus, Freemasons, or countless professional and social bodies that constitute the phenomenon known as the old boy network. Because an invitation to attend a Bilderberg meeting carries with it the allure of meeting sites in foreign locales that have five-star hotels affording privacy, access to golf courses, and facilities offering other luxurious amenities, the requirement that the attendees personally pay their expenses and "sing for their supper" by speaking for a few minutes, is a small price to pay for the flattery of being counted among the world's elite.

If David Rockefeller felt that being a Bilderberger established his "credibility," it must have been a tremendous boost to the ego of a relatively unknown member of the U.S. Congress, Britain's House of Commons, government official, businessman, journalist, or a small-state governor, such as Bill Clinton, to be invited, and to know that whatever was said would remain a secret.

No one is more protective of confidentiality than the second-most famous member of the Bilderberg Group. Although an article in *The New York Times* on April 30, 1989, by Jeff Gerth with Sarah Bartlett, titled "Kissinger and Friends and Revolving Doors," did not deal with the Bilderberg Group, it demonstrated the relationships between influential international figures that lend weight to assertions that members of the Bilderberg Group, the CFR, and the Trilateral Commission are part of a scheme to establish a "New World Order" global government. Noting that two of Kissinger's senior colleagues in Kissinger's consulting firm are Brent Scowcroft and Lawrence S. Eagleburger [both are Bilderbergers}, the article stated, "Through their close relationships with foreign governments and their extensive knowledge of foreign affairs, they have made a very good living by offering geopolitical insight, advice and entree to about 30 leading global companies. Among those willing to pay $200,000 or more to be clients of Kissinger Associates are ITT, American Express, Anheuser-Busch, Coca-Cola, H. J. Heinz [H. J. Heinz III was a Bilderberger], Fiat [its founder, Giovanni Agnelli was a Bilderberger], Volvo, L. M. Ericsson, Daewoo and Midland Bank."

In a field as subtle as foreign policy, asked Gerth and Bartlett, can people like Mr. Kissinger and his associates wall off what they know of confidential government discussions from what they can legitimately advise their corporate clients? And when people of their stature help shape government decisions, can they ignore what they know of their corporate clients' interests?

"The Kissinger group," the article noted, "is a prominent instance of a pervasive Washington phenomenon: the 'revolving door.' Mr. Scowcroft now serves President Bush as national security adviser, a post he had previously held under President Gerald R. Ford, succeeding Mr. Kissinger. And Mr. Eagleburger, who served as undersecretary of state before becoming president of Kissinger Associates in 1984, recently stepped up to deputy secretary, the department's No. 2 position. The jobs are among the most sensitive and influential in Washington. Mr. Scowcroft briefs President Bush on pressing diplomatic and military matters, and Mr. Eagleburger helps formulate the administration's strategy for East–West relations and other leading issues.

"Kissinger and Scowcroft, as frequent unpaid members of federal advisory boards, counseled President Reagan on arms control issues at the same time that they worked for clients involved in missile systems and missile making.

"From two discreet, unmarked offices in New York and Washington," Gerth and Bartlett wrote, "more than 20 staff members of Kissinger Associates work on research and analysis for the presentations, mostly oral, that Mr. Kissinger and his colleagues make to their clients. For his efforts, Mr. Eagleburger earned a total of $674,000 last year, $214,000 of which was paid by Kent Associates, an affiliate of the company that handles more specific assignments. Mr. Scowcroft made $293,000 as a consultant to Kissinger Associates. What exactly do they do for that much money?

"An executive from H. J. Heinz [its founder was a Bilderberger] said that Kissinger helped provide background and introductions when the company was considering building a baby food factory in China. And an executive at the Swedish bank Skandinaviska Enskilda Banken, a former client, attributed its early sell-off of Latin American loans to Kissinger's insights.

"Little is known about what Kissinger Associates does for its clients." The firm does not have an Internet address, and Kissinger refuses to name its clients.

In a profile of Kissinger and his firm in 1986, *Time* magazine noted, "The expertise and access gained in years of power are carefully nurtured, valuable commodities, to be marketed now through Kissinger Associates, his international consulting firm. It is widely regarded as the Tiffany of that arcane new business known as corporate risk analysis, a growth industry in today's turbulent world. His firm consists of only nine advisers and researchers, a far cry from the 12,000 under his command at the State Department. The senior members are longtime Kissinger colleagues—and protégés—who bring their own distinction: former undersecretary of state Lawrence Eagleburger and retired general Brent Scowcroft, who was Kissinger's deputy and then successor as National Security Adviser. But what sets this firm apart from others is Kissinger, who retains his clout even though he was frozen out by the Reagan administration. Kissinger is sole owner of the firm, which grosses an estimated $5 million a year."

At his Park Avenue office, noted *Time*, Kissinger worked "at a desk covered with precise rows of labeled folders, suggesting a world tidier than it is. Gone are the old trappings of office—the direct phone link to the president, the reams of classified documents. But he dismisses secret papers as too short-range to be useful now. Experience enables his team to glean much from press reports. He is out more than in, meeting clients in corporate boardrooms, making more than 50 speeches a year for a minimum of $20,000 each, cultivating new contacts as old ones phase out.

"Furio Colombo, the president of Fiat, USA, explained why his parent company, which built airplane engines, agricultural equipment and airports as well as automobiles, turned to Kissinger Associates: 'He understands not just the external factors but the company's inside way of thinking, the different kinds of products, different cultural needs. He is both flexible and deep, two things that don't come together easily.' "

When Fiat chairman Giovanni Agnelli flew "from Italy, Kissinger had been known to call his wife Nancy and have an extra place set at their next dinner party. The president of one U.S.-based company said that Kissinger not only offered a valuable geopolitical analysis of the world but also provided valuable entree and contacts to government and business leaders around the world."

Noting that Kissinger "bridles when rivals suggest that he trades on his name and contacts," *Time* reported that Kissinger retorted, "We are not door openers. Everywhere I have traveled in the past year, the heads of governments received me. I do not ask them to do a favor for a client, and I don't bring clients in with me. Some time ago a foreign company offered me one million dollars, to be deposited in a Swiss bank the minute the company chairman walked through the door of a certain important finance minister. It would have required one phone call. The minister was a close personal friend. I turned it down."

Kissinger also scoffed at critics who say the clients are buying the name.

"Nobody continues paying you for your name," he said. "You either do something they can justify to their boards, or they drop you."

In addition to his role as "diplomat-for-hire, lecturer and special commentator for ABC," *Time* recorded, "Kissinger composes a newspaper column every month for the *Los Angeles Times* syndicate. While the column, carried by *The Washington Post*, is vintage Kissinger in its grand sweep and magisterial voice, his careful avoidance of direct criticism of the administration has made it less trenchant—and less influential—than it might otherwise be. It all adds up to a life that is both lucrative and satisfying.

"When the Senate Foreign Relations Committee first tried to elicit more information on Kissinger Associates activities as part of the confirmation process, Eagleburger 'was adamant in his refusal' to discuss any details, according to a committee staff member. He invoked a confidentiality clause in the firm's contracts that prohibits any discussion of its contractual arrangements unless mandated by law.... He later provided a general description of some of the advice the firm gave most clients. The committee declined to push him for more details, and he was unanimously confirmed.... Kissinger said that he and his colleagues went to great lengths to avoid any conflicts and to keep their policy recommendations separate from their business interests. Neither he nor his associates, he said, will work on behalf of any government. Nor, he added, does any person from the firm lobby American officials on behalf of a client."

For the five years prior to 1989, Kissinger had a window into the government's most sensitive information as a member of the president's Foreign Intelligence Advisory Board. "The 16-member board is a little-known but powerful group of scientists, business executives and former government officials," many of them Bilderbergers, "that gives independent advice about a wide range of intelligence issues and activities. Some of the board's other prominent members are William French Smith, a former attorney general, and Zbigniew Brzezinski [a Bilderberger], the national security adviser to President Jimmy Carter.

"'There are all sorts of conflicts on the board,' said Anne L. Armstrong, chairman of the board and a former ambassador, but she added, 'It comes down to believing in your board members' integrity.'

"Kissinger said he had not excused himself from discussing any matter before the advisory board, nor had he participated in any board matter in which, 'to his knowledge, he has a financial interest.'

"Kissinger said that his principal area of involvement at the intelligence advisory board had been arms control and that he saw no conflict because none of his clients were really involved in arms control matters. But public records showed that some clients of Kissinger Associates were affected by military matters. For example, one client, the ITT

Corporation, a $9 billion corporation with about seven percent of its annual business in military contracts, operated various United States missile systems under a $700 million contract, according to annual company reports. Eagleburger was an ITT director for the previous four years, and told the Senate committee about cost problems with ITT's missile contracts."

A former official of the president's Foreign Intelligence Advisory Board, who asked not to be identified because of the board's secrecy pledge, said that Kissinger, using his authority as a board member, frequently reviewed intelligence documents outside the regular board meetings. In addition, the former official said he believed that Kissinger's association with the board gave him benefit because he could not have separated the insights gained from his access to United States intelligence data from his analysis and advice to clients.

In addition to the Foreign Intelligence Advisory Board, Kissinger worked on a number of other government advisory bodies, including a 1983 presidential commission on strategic forces headed by Scowcroft. Its principal mandate was to recommend alternative locations for the MX missile. At the time, Scowcroft was president of Kissinger Associates as well as a personal consultant on general arms control and military issues for Lockheed Corporation.

Raising the topic of the secrecy of the Kissinger Associates client list in an interview with Kissinger on CNN, correspondent Wolf Blitzer quoted a *Los Angeles Times* editorial that stated, "His company, Kissinger Associates, is known for introducing U.S. firms looking for business overseas to leaders of foreign governments. The company has not disclosed all of its clients or detailed the work it does. There is the possibility of a conflict of interest in investigating foreign governments that can be beneficial to clients." Blitzer asked, "What about that point, that your company, Kissinger Associates, does not disclose its clients and there could be potentially a conflict of interest?"

Kissinger replied, "No law firm discloses its clients. I will discuss my clients fully with the counsel of the White House and with the appropriate ethics groups. And the possibility that the investigation of a commission that contains eight commissioners would be affected by any conceived commercial interests is outrageous. I have served six presidents, and I have never been accused of anything of this kind."

In a letter to President George W. Bush on May 2, 1991, the chairman of the House Committee on Finance and Urban Affairs, Henry Gonzalez wrote:

"The House Banking Committee is conducting an investigation into over $4 billion in unreported loans the former employees of the Atlanta branch of Banca Nazionale del Lavoro (BNL) provided to the government of Iraq between 1985 and 1990. The Committee's investigation has uncovered the fact that Henry Kissinger was on the International Advisory Board of BNL during that same time period and that BNL was a client of Kissinger Associates.

"As you are aware, Mr. Brent Scowcroft and Mr. Lawrence Eagleburger were high ranking officials of Kissinger Associates—Mr. Scowcroft as vice chairman and Mr. Eagleburger as president. Kissinger Associates represents many large multinational companies involved in various aspects of international trade, including the arms business. Since these firms sell their wares worldwide, they often are the beneficiaries of U.S. policy towards foreign countries. I am deeply concerned over the potential influence Mr. Kissinger may exert over the decisions and actions of Mr. Scowcroft and Mr. Eagleburger, and am especially troubled by a potential conflict of interest involving Mr. Scowcroft."

Gonzalez continued, "The National Security Advisor is in a position to strongly influence our national security and foreign policies, including the U.S. export licensing process. These policies often have a direct influence on individual corporations doing business abroad. Until October 4, 1990, Mr. Scowcroft owned stock in approximately 40 U.S. corporations, many of which were doing business in Iraq. Those companies received more than one out of every eight U.S. export licenses for exports to Iraq. Several of the companies were also clients of Kissinger Associates while Mr. Scowcroft was vice chairman of that firm.

"Mr. Scowcroft's stock holdings, particularly in corporations that are clients of Kissinger Associates, present the potential for serious conflicts of interest and cause one to question whether or not his decisions as National Security Advisor are completely disassociated from the interests of his former boss and longtime colleague."

The letter further noted, "Mr. Eagleburger, the current deputy secretary of state, as well as Mr. Scowcroft, may also be involved in a conflict of interest related to their role in promoting military sales abroad. The *Legal Times* recently reported that Mr. Eagleburger and Mr. Scowcroft (a lifelong Air Force officer) are strong advocates of using $1 billion in Export-Import Bank resources to finance the sale of U.S. military articles overseas."

Gonzalez asserted that Scowcroft's and Eagleburger's actions "seem out of step at a time when the U.S. should be leading a worldwide effort to limit arms proliferation. The positions held by these men are of the utmost importance to the national security of the United States. Persons filling such important positions must be independent from past associations which could cloud their judgment."

Despite Kissinger's denial of conflicts of interest, those who believe that he is part of the Bilderberg Group's conspiracy to bring about a New World Order controlled by bankers and global corporations claim that they have been motivated by profit.

In October 2004, Kissinger Associates and APCO Worldwide announced that they had formed "a strategic alliance." Kissinger stated, "Our grasp of core policy and regulatory issues in numerous countries combined with APCO's extensive public affairs experience will result in well-rounded thinking about our clients' challenges. I am confident that this kind of thinking will produce very exciting and productive results for the corporations we both serve. In today's global marketplace, the needs of multinational organizations are more complicated than ever. These needs are inevitably shaped by the diverse regulatory, political and public opinion landscapes in these countries. This alliance will create a team whose ability to understand and affect these environments will be second to none."

The announcement stated that Alan R. Batkin [member of Trilateral Commission and a Bilderberger] and J. Stapleton Roy [Bilderberger] would be active in the alliance. Batkin was a former investment banker and leader in international business who served on boards and executive committees of a number of think tanks and publicly traded companies. Roy was a former ambassador to Singapore, Indonesia, and the People's Republic of China who also served as assistant secretary of state for intelligence and research.

While Bilderberg observers such as Daniel Estulin, Jim Tucker, and Tony Gosling look at Kissinger's business affairs and Bilderberg attendance and discern in the secrecy surrounding them with evidence of conspiracies, they appear to others as nothing more than the old boy network, but on an international scale. While conspiracists see sinister aspects in the overlapping memberships of Bilderberg, the CFR, Trilateral Commission, and Bohemian Grove, others find nothing unusual or alarming.

The diversity of the Bilderberg's old boy network was demonstrated in an *Ottawa Citizen* story about the Group's 2006 meeting in Canada. Along with Kissinger and Vernon Jordan were other participants:

Andrzej Olechowski: A former minister of foreign affairs and finance in his native Poland, he ran unsuccessfully in the 2000 presidential election and Warsaw's 2002 mayoral race. He was a founding member of the centrist Civic Platform party and eurrently a member of the supervisory boards of Vivendi Universal, Citibank Handlowy and PKN Orlen.

Egil Myklebust: Served as president and CEO of Norsk Hydro, a

Norwegian oil and gas group, one of that country's biggest companies, between 1991 and 2001. He then served as Norsk's chairman until 2004 and was a member of the World Business Council for Sustainable Development. He is currently chairman of Scandinavian Airlines.

Robert Zoellick, U.S. deputy secretary of state: A lawyer, worked in economic and diplomatic policy development in different Republican administrations, with a strong reputation for hammering out international trade deals. He played a key role in creating NAFTA and was an important figure in World Trade Organization talks.

James B. Steinberg: Best known for his work as deputy national security adviser to President Bill Clinton from 1996 to 2000, he went on to direct foreign policy studies at the Brookings Institution in Washington and is dean of the Lyndon B. Johnson School of Public Affairs at the University of Texas at Austin. A frequent media commentator on foreign policy, he had written several books on national security topics.

Juan Luis Cebrian: The CEO of the Spanish media conglomerate Grupa Prisa, which owns *El Pais*, a center-left daily that is the country's leading newspaper. A former editor at the newspaper, he also served as chairman of the International Press Institute.

Mario Monti: Dubbed "Super Mario" by the press, he was an Italian economist, president of Bocconi University in Milan and chairman of the European think tank Bruegel. He most notably served on the European Commission, where he was sometimes called an antitrust czar. He fought against a proposed merger between General Electric and Honeywell in 2001. The European Union eventually blocked that merger, earning criticism from U.S. regulators. Reported to be a Bilderberger.

Jean-Pierre Hansen: CEO of energy giants Electrabel, Belgium's main power producer, and Suez-Tractebel, Belgium's top utility holding company and one of the world's biggest independent power producers. Hansen earned advanced degrees in engineering and economics and worked in the electricity and gas sectors since the 1970s.

Neelie Kroes: A veteran Dutch politician and businesswoman who had served as European Commissioner for Competition since 2004. Since assuming her post, she was in the middle of Microsoft's dispute with the EU over a 2004 antitrust ruling against the company.

Franco Bernabe: Vice chairman of the European investment bank Rothschild Europe, former CEO of the Italian energy giant ENI and a board member of Petro-China, he headed ENI's privatization process in the early 1990s. He worked as a chief economist at Fiat, and started his career as an academic at Turin University.

Frank McKenna: Canada's ambassador to the U.S. under Prime Minister Paul Martin. When Martin left office, he returned to private life, quickly quelling rumors he would run for the Liberal Party leadership. Before his ambassadorship, he practiced law and served on numerous corporate boards. He became New Brunswick's premier in 1987, winning every seat. He served for a decade and created a call center industry in the resource-based province.

Jorma Ollila: Served as chairman and CEO of Nokia Corporation for fourteen years. He became nonexecutive chairman of Royal Dutch Shell while maintaining his Nokia association as nonexecutive chairman. The first non-Dutch, non-Briton to head Shell, he took Nokia from a cell phone company on the brink of takeover to the world's most successful firm in the field. He was a member of the board of directors of Ford Motor Company.

Richard Perle: Assistant secretary of defense to President Ronald Reagan, he was an advisor to President George W. Bush, serving as chairman of the Defense Policy Board from 2001–2003. He had been assistant secretary of defense for international security policy (1981–1987). His op-ed columns appeared regularly in *The*

New York Times, The Wall Street Journal and London's *Daily Telegraph.* A
Bilderberg regular.

James Wolfensohn: President of the World Bank, he was born in Australia
and ended up on Wall Street via London, eventually founding a
banking firm with former head of the U.S. Federal Reserve. He
was credited with working to return the World Bank to its original
mandate of relieving poverty. A Bilderberger.

John Vinocur: A senior correspondent for the *International Herald Tribune,*
he reports on everything from politics to sports. He went to the
Tribune from *The New York Times,* where he was metropolitan editor.
He served as the *Times* bureau chief in France and Germany. He
went to the *Tribune* as executive editor and served as the newspaper's
vice president from 1986–1996. He also wrote for *Foreign Affairs*
and *The New York Times Magazine.* A Bilderberger.

Adrian Wooldridge: Washington bureau chief of *The Economist,* he had been
the magazine's West Coast correspondent and also held positions
as its management correspondent and its correspondent in Britain.
He is co-author of *A Future Perfect: The Challenge and Hidden Promise of
Globalization* and *The Right Nation,* a look at American conservatism. A
Bilderberger.

Dermot Gleeson: Chairman of Allied Irish Banks, a lawyer, member of
the Royal Irish Academy and chairman of the Irish Council for
Bioethics, he had been attorney general of Ireland. He also served
as a member of the Council of State for Ireland and as then Irish
prime minister John Bruton's chief legal adviser (1994–1997). He
joined the board of Allied Irish Banks in 2000 and was appointed
chairman in 2003.

At the Bilderberg meeting, held in Istanbul, Turkey, from May 31
to June 3, being in the presence of old boy network luminaries proved
exciting to one of Turkey's leading journalists, authors, and TV com-
mentators, Mehmet Ali Birand. Born in 1941, he started his career in

1964 with one of the country's leading newspapers, *Milliyet*. In 1972 he became its European editor, followed by Moscow Bureau Chief in 1984. In 1985, he started producing and narrating the program *32nd Day*. A broadcast about national and international issues, the program continued airing for twenty years. In 1991, he started writing as a columnist in the newspaper *Sabah*, and in 1999 in *Posta Newspaper*, the highest circulated newspaper in Turkey. Through 1999–2005, he prepared and narrated a daily political talk-show. *Mansset* (Headline) on CNN Turk. In 2006 he became the anchorman of *Kanal D*. He reported on several conferences on Turkey's relationship with the EU, Cyprus and Turkey–Greece relations. Given Turkey's "Best Reporter" award, he was also a recipient of "Chevalier de l'Ordre National de Merite."

In an account of his experiences at Bilderberg 2007 for *Turkish Daily News*, Mehmet wrote, "It took place under extensive secrecy and security. We were confined to the Ritz Carlton Hotel. There were nearly one hundred participants. No one else was allowed into the hotel; not even one single outsider was let in. We went to sleep, got up, ate at the same place and held meetings one after the other from 8 A.M. until 6 P.M. My head was full of questions before going into the meetings. The identities of the attendees were known beforehand. They were all very prominent people. What could have happened when so many famous and important people got together?"

After settling in his room, Mehmet wore his best suit, put on his most stylish tie, and went down to the meeting room. His excitement intensified when he looked around and saw that he was surrounded by people who almost constantly made it in newspaper and television headlines. Letting what he called "the tide of Bilderberg" carry him away, he felt a "need to participate, ask questions, and watch attentively."

Everyone took the meetings seriously. No one left sessions to go outside, or to stroll around, or have coffee. After three days, Mehmet looked at his notes and was disappointed.

"Where were the secret decisions?" he asked. "Where were the conspiracy theories? And were there not supposed to be decisions made about presidential elections and a coup attempt? Where?

"There were neither secret plans made, nor secrets uttered, nor secret decisions taken. It was no different than hundreds of other high-end international conferences he'd attended, except for the influential participants.

"On the other hand," he wrote, "it was heaven for someone interested in international relations, just like myself. I learned a lot. We started at the developments in Iraq and went on to discuss China's place in the world. Would it be a single-polar world, or a multi-polar one? How Iran's nuclear power would affect all of us was discussed in detail.

"Concerns on the issue were conveyed. The developments in the United States, what the elections would bring, and how the public opinion in the United States was progressing were deliberated."

The most important issues facing the world, from energy policies to expansion in the communication technologies, were reviewed. At the end of the three days, Mehmet said, he had learned and discussed "the world's most prominent problems with the world's experts."

At a Saturday night cocktail party during the 2005 meeting at the luxurious Dorint Sofitel Seehotel Überfahrt several Bilderbergers had shared conversations standing at the bar with Queen Beatrix of Holland and Donald Graham, CEO of *The Washington Post*, discussing aspects of a pending sale of Spanish telecommunications and cable giant Auna, operator of fixed-line telephone services, a mobile-phone network, and a cable television system.

The first day of Bilderberg 2005 in Rottach-Egern, Germany, was dominated by talk of the EU Constitutional referendum in France and whether President Jacques Chirac would be able to persuade France to vote yes on May 29. According to sources within Bilderberg, a yes vote would put a lot of pressure on Prime Minister Tony Blair to deliver a positive result in a referendum on the EU treaty scheduled for 2006.

"Bilderbergers hoped that Blair and Chirac . . . could work together for their mutual benefit and political survival." A European Bilderberger urged both leaders to "put behind them as quickly as possible all past disputes on such topics as Iraq and the liberalization of Europe's economy." A German attendee wondered how Blair should go about convincing Britons to embrace the European Constitution when Britain's economy was doing well, while EU member Germany and France were suffering 10 percent unemployment.

Bilderberg 2005 was missing one of its luminaries, U.S. State Department official John Bolton who was testifying before the Senate Foreign Relations Committee, so the American government was represented "by Allan Hubbard, assistant to the president for economic policy and director of the National Economic Council; William Luti, the deputy undersecretary of defense; James Wolfensohn, outgoing president of the World Bank; and Paul Wolfowitz, deputy secretary of state."

What all students and writers of history discover about momentous events in the political affairs of the world is that they are the result of intensely personal relationships, such as Roosevelt's with Churchill, Reagan and Thatcher, and Reagan and Gorbachev. After Saddam Hussein's forces invaded Kuwait, Thatcher told President George H. W. Bush that the United States must act militarily. "George," she said, "this is no time to go wobbly."

In a scene in the film *The Day of the Jackal*, the chief of Scotland Yard's Special Branch finds himself awakened in the middle of the night by a telephone call from a French detective who is tracking an assassin who might be English. After the call, the Scotland Yard chief's wife asks, "Who was that?"

He replies sleepily, "The old boy network."

Long before the Bilderberg Group, the CFR, and the Trilateral Commission, what President Herbert Hoover once called "the greatest men's party on Earth" was formed by a group of San Francisco journalists. An annual all-male gathering near the Russian River was first held in 1879. Called the Bohemian Club, its membership is coveted, and people who want to belong routinely wait ten or fifteen years before gaining admittance. There are currently about 2,700 members. Like Bilderberg and the Trilateral Commission, the club has drawn criticism because of its emphasis on privacy. Like Bilderberg, the presence of powerful men gathered in secrecy has inspired visions of a conspiracy to rule the world. Philip Weiss of *Spy Magazine* reported that in 1989 the Bohemian Grove drew notables such as former president George H. W. Bush; his son, Texas governor George W. Bush; Henry Kissinger; retired general Colin Powell; former house speaker Newt Gingrich; and Dow Chemical chairman Frank Popoff. On December 26, 1987, *The Economist* called Bohemian Grove a "concentration of big cheeses, tycoons (nearby Santa Rosa airport is jammed with executive jets), leading academics, lawyers, entertainers, and politicians (particularly Republican ones).... Movers and shakers enjoy the Bohemian Grove for its informality (old clothes, no ties), relaxation (long walks in the 2,700 wooded acres, swimming in the Russian River), entertainment (no televisions, hi-fis or radios, but music all day long), drink and excellent food."

"The men gathered to celebrate what they called 'the spirit of Bohemia,'" said Peter Phillips, a Sonoma State University sociology professor who wrote his doctoral dissertation on the Bohemian Club.

Weiss wrote, "The fiercely guarded, 2,700-acre retreat is the country extension of San Francisco's all-male ultra-exclusive Bohemian Club to which every Republican president since Herbert Hoover has belonged."

Admission is by invitation, and those who receive one must be recommended by a member. Club bylaws have stated that a member-sponsor's application "shall be in writing and shall contain full information for the guidance" of the Board in determining the merits and the qualifications of the proposed guest."

"You know you are inside the Bohemian Grove," Weiss wrote, "when you come down a trail in the woods and hear piano music from amid a group of tents and then round a bend to see a man with a beer in one hand and his penis in the other, urinating into the bushes. This is the most gloried-in ritual of the encampment, the freedom of powerful men to pee wherever they like, a right the club has invoked when trying to fight government anti-sex discrimination efforts and one curtailed only when it comes to a few popular redwoods just outside the Dining Circle.

"Everything in the encampment is sheltered by redwoods, which admit hazy shafts of sunlight, and every camp has a more or less constant campfire sending a soft column of smoke into the trees. The walled camps are generally about 100 feet wide and stretch back up the hillside, with wooden platforms on which members set up tents. Bohemians sleep on cots in these tents, or, in the richer camps, in redwood cabins. The camps are decorated with wooden or stone sculptures of owls, the Grove symbol. Members wash up in dormitory-style bathrooms and eat breakfast and dinner collectively in the Dining Circle, an outdoor arena with fresh wood chips covering the ground and only the sky above."

Weiss noted that the sense of being in "an actual club was heightened by furnishings that could not survive a wet season outdoors: a stuffed lion, red lanterns in the trees at night adding to a haunting atmosphere, paintings of camels and naked women that are hung outside . . . and everywhere pianos that, when the encampment ended, went back to a piano warehouse near the front gate. There was always a feeling of both rusticity and great privilege."

Although the Carlyle Group is not an organization of powerful men who meet every year in a posh resort wrapped in secrecy, it has come to symbolize the globalization that has alarmed the Bilderberg watchers. Based in Washington, DC, the Carlyle Group described itself as one of the world's largest private equity firms, with more than $81.1 billion under management with sixty funds across four investment disciplines (buyouts, venture and growth capital, real estate and leveraged finance). The firm's website noted that it combined "global vision with local insight, relying on a topflight team of 575 investment professionals" operating out of offices in more than twenty countries "to uncover superior opportunities in North America, Europe, Asia, Australia, the Middle East/North Africa and Latin America."

Journalist Tim Shorrock noted in *The Nation* on March 14, 2002, "By hiring enough former officials to fill a permanent shadow cabinet, Carlyle has brought political influence to a new level and created a twenty-first-century version of capitalism that blurs any line between politics and business. In a sense, Carlyle may be the ultimate in privatization: the use of a private company to nurture public policy—and then reap its benefits in the form of profit. Although the fund claims to operate like any other investment bank, said Shorrock, it was undeniable that its stable of statesmen-entrepreneurs have the ability to tap into networks in government and commerce, both at home and abroad, for advance intelligence about companies about to be sold and spun off, or government budgets and policies about to be implemented, and then transform that knowledge into investment strategies that dovetail nicely with United States military foreign and domestic policy."

The managing director of the Center for Public Integrity, a non-profit Washington, DC think tank, Peter Eisner, said, "It should be a deep cause for concern that a closely held company like Carlyle can simultaneously have directors and advisers that are doing business and making money and also advising the president of the United States. The problem comes when private business and public policy blend together."

• **Seventeen** •

Bilderberg and the New World Order

On the sixty-fourth anniversary of the D-Day landings at Normandy, France, that began the liberation of Europe after five years of Nazi rule, Bilderberg Group regulars and a few first-timers met in the United States. For the second time in six years, they convened at the Westfields Marriott hotel in Chantilly, Virginia. Evoking the style and charm of colonial estates, it provided sophisticated conference facilities, elegant accommodations, and exciting resort activities, including the National Air and Space Museum, the Manassas (Bull Run) Civil War battlefield, and Wolf Trap Center for Performing Arts.

Just seven miles from Washington Dulles International Airport and only thirty minutes from Washington DC, the hotel offered "335 guest rooms, including eight suites, two-line cordless phones, minibars, hair dryers, Internet access, voice mail, cable television, spa with whirlpool, sauna, health club, lighted tennis courts, biking and jogging trails," swimming pool (indoor/outdoor), "and an eighteen-hole championship golf course designed by Fred Couples." There were three restaurants, including the Palm Court (formal upscale dining), Wellington's Pub (casual British pub atmosphere), Fairfax Dining Room (especially for conference attendees), and in-house Starbucks or Westfield's Lounge.

"There were a 40,000-square-foot conference center with 28 meeting rooms, the largest of which seated 600; three ballrooms; amphitheater' production studio; and state-of-the-art audio and video facilities with a full-production, fiber-optic capability."

From Thursday, June 5, to Sunday, June 8, 2008, all of this was reserved for the Bilderbergers. As they arrived in cars and limousines with darkened windows, they passed by a few small clusters of protestors holding up placards and shouting against perceived threats to individual liberty, national sovereignty, and the dollar, and creation of a New World Order. In the days leading up to the meeting, the Internet blossomed with speculation, rumors, and wildly imaginable suppositions. With news reports that Hillary Clinton was in Washington and about to end her campaign for the Democratic presidential nomination, and that she might meet with Senator Barack Obama to acknowledge his victory and endorse him, speculation was rife that they would drop in on the Group's meeting at Chantilly.

Paul Joseph Watson wrote for PrisonPlanet that they "went out of their way to hold their long-awaited private meeting in a very specific location, not at Hillary's mansion in Washington, but in Northern Virginia, which also just happens to be the scene of the 2008 Bilderberg meeting."

When the Associated Press reported that journalists traveling with Obama "sensed something might be happening between the pair when they arrived at Dulles International Airport after an event in Northern Virginia and Obama was not aboard the airplane," the Bilderberg watchers noted that "Dulles just happens to be walking distance from the Westfields Marriott."

The website Wonkette stated, "Guess who had a very private talky-talk in Northern Virginia tonight, probably at the Bilderberg Group meeting in Chantilly? Your Barack Obama and Hillary Clinton! They really met and talked, in private, Thursday night. And really, it sounds like they did this at that creepy Bilderberg Group meeting, which is happening now, and which is so secret that nobody will admit they're going, even though everybody who is anybody goes to Bilderberg."

Obama and Clinton did meet, but at the home of California senator Dianne Feinstein. Asserting that both Clinton and Obama "have
deep rooted connections to the Bilderberg elitists," and as mentioned
earlier, one writer noted that Bill Clinton attended the 1991 meeting
in Germany shortly before he was elected president, and Hillary Clinton was said to have attended the 2006 meeting in Ottawa, Canada.
Also noted was the attendance at Bilderberg 2008 of James A. (Jim)
Johnson, head of the Federal National Mortgage Association (Fannie Mae), who had been named by Obama to screen potential Obama
running mates. Noting that Johnson also selected John Kerry's running
mate, John Edwards, in 2004 after Edwards greatly impressed a Bilderberg meeting in Italy that year, the item added that Johnson attended
the 2006 meeting in Turkey and belonged to the American Friends of
Bilderberg, "an offshoot group that organizes the Bilderberg Group's
annual meeting."

Judi McLeod of *Canada Free Press* wrote, "Although coming on like a
freight train as the 'Messiah For Change,' Barack Obama's just another
poodle of the power brokers when it comes to who will be his Veep.
[It's] the big boys who will decide who fills that slot. Bilderbergers pull
the puppet strings of contemporary politicians. While the media tends
to present Bilderberger luminaries as bigwigs in pinstripe suits attending endless secret meetings, they're the global elitists pushing the enve-
lope on one-world government.... Barack Obama may look like the
Messiah For Change when in reality he's just another Bilderberg Boy."

In an unusual mention of Bilderberg, *The Washington Post* in its June
10 story about Johnson's appointment stated that he was "a member
of exclusive clubs such as American Friends of Bilderberg, the Trilateral
Commission and the Council on Foreign Relations." Two days later,
Johnson was back in the headlines. After *The Wall Street Journal* revealed
that he had received mortgages worth more than seven million dollars,
including at least two loans below market average, from Countrywide
Financial, a firm that was at the heart of a collapse of the mortgage

business, the article noted that the transactions may have been perfectly aboveboard, but "several could prove too cozy," depending on how much they overlapped with Johnson's position at Fannie Mae. "There is nothing illegal about a mortgage firm treating some borrowers better than others," the *Journal* article noted. "But if Fannie Mae officials received special treatment, that could cause a political problem for the government-sponsored, shareholder-owned company."

After Republicans in the John McCain campaign pounced on the revelation, Johnson resigned from Obama's vice-presidential search committee.

As usual, Jim Tucker and Alex Jones were on hand at Chantilly. Immediately before Jones was to be interviewed by phone on a nationally syndicated broadcast hosted by George Noory on the night before the Bilderberg meeting was to begin, a fire alarm sounded, forcing an evacuation of the hotel. "I know this is a setup," Jones said. "They timed this exactly. The moment the phone rang the alarm goes off. They want to use this to flush us out of here. We come in here, the phone rings, and right as the phone rings this alarm goes off."

He also claimed that FBI agents had "grilled him and Tucker" on whether they were planning anything violent. "There's agents and spies everywhere. Everywhere we go we are followed. . . . They are questioning us, getting in our faces," said Jones. "We're reporters, it's our right when 120 world leaders show up, we have a right and a duty to find out what's going on."

Paul Joseph Warren wrote, "Since the U.S. corporate media has steadfastly refused to utter one word on 125 power brokers meeting in secret to discuss the future of the planet, it is not only the duty but the necessity of the alternative media to fill the hole and keep Americans informed about what is taking place this week in Chantilly. If 125 film stars booked out a hotel, arrived in dark-tinted limousines and met in secret, do you think the corporate media would be interested in finding out what they were there to discuss? Yet 125 top CEOs, hugely influential philanthropists, heads of state, NATO officials, academic leaders, banking kingpins, and European royalty—the very people that shape the destiny of the world—can get together for three days without a single U.S. corporate media outlet reporting on it."

Asserting that "you certainly won't read about it in *The Washington Post, The New York Times* or *The Wall Street Journal*, since the editors of those three newspapers are all Bilderberg members," Warren wrote. "This is why Tucker and Jones are forced to undergo harassment and scrutiny almost every year merely for covering the event, because not one mainstream media outlet dares to break ranks with its elite owners and undertake real investigative journalism."

In addition to American regulars Rockefeller, Kissinger, Richard Perle, Henry Kravis, Vernon Jordan, Paul Gigot of *The Wall Street Journal*, Donald Graham of *The Washington Post* company, and Paul Wolfowitz, the list of Chantilly attendees included Secretary of State Condoleeza Rice, Treasury Secretary Henry Paulson, former Reagan administration official George Shultz, Eric Schmidt (CEO of Google), public television talk-show host Charlie Rose, Kansas governor Kathleen Sebelius (mentioned as a possible Obama running mate), Federal Reserve Board chairman Ben S. Bernanke, and the chief of the supersecret intelligence-gathering National Security Agency (NSA), Keith B. Alexander. Created in secrecy in 1952 by President Harry S. Truman, the NSA grew into the nation's largest intelligence agency, operating spy satellites and intercepting electronic communications to screen them for threats to U.S. security. Providing far more insight on foreign countries than the CIA and other spy organizations, it has been jokingly referred to as "No Such Agency." Because its original target had been the Communist bloc, it wrapped the Soviet Union and its satellite nations in an electronic cocoon. Anytime an aircraft, ship, or military unit moved, the NSA would know. From 22,300 miles in orbit, satellites with super-thin, football-field-sized antennas eavesdropped on Soviet communications and weapons signals. After Muslim terrorists attacked the World Trade Center towers and the Pentagon on September 11, 2001, the agency became an even more vital part of the intelligence system.

One of the beliefs that spread among Bilderberg watchers was that information which NSA analysts collected, with the help of the CIA, Drug Enforcement Agency, and FBI, on prospective Bilderberg attendees, was given to the Steering Committee, which shared the information with Trilateral Commission membership screeners.

As the 2008 conference at Chantilly adjourned, and Bilderbergers dispersed in their limousines and SUVs with darkened windows, Jim Tucker was reporting that his unnamed sources inside the "meeting had leaked details of what elitists were discussing."

Under the heading of resisting terrorism, Tucker claimed, were points about how the terrorist organizations are recruiting people who do not look like terrorists. Ominously, the anonymous source also told Tucker that Bilderbergers were discussing the microchipping of humans on a mass scale, which would be introduced "under the pretext of fighting terrorism whereby the 'good guys' would be allowed to travel freely from airports so long as their microchip could be scanned and the information stored in a database. Tucker said the idea was also sold on the basis that it would help hospital staff treat a patient in an emergency situation because a scan of the chip would provide instantaneous access to health details."

These discussions were said to have taken place "in a main conference hall and was part of the agenda, not an off-hand remark in the hotel bar."

Tucker's source was reported to have "told him that Secretary of Defense Robert Gates attended Bilderberg despite him not appearing on the official list. Tucker said that sources told him Gates was in attendance to present his case for war with Iran, but that the majority of Bilderberg members were against an attack at that time."

"The Europeans were generally opposed to an invasion of Iran," said

Tucker, adding that European Bilderbergers made "snide comments about where such nuclear weapons actually were being kept and at one point joking that they were possibly 'in Saddam Hussein's tomb.' " He said that most Americans present at the meeting were opposed to an attack on Iran, but dared not be as visible and loud in their opposition as the Europeans."

When the meeting ended, a protestor reported that the Fairfax County police, Secret Service, armed private security, and "other protectors of the global elite" had guarded each entranceway. Radio personality, filmmaker and perennial Bilderberg watcher Alex Jones was present, as were "We Are Change" and the "9-11 Truth Movement," carrying placards and signs. At least two bullhorns blasted "the moneyed guests planning" the nation's future in the hotel. There were a number of people wearing "Ron Paul Revolution" and "9-11 Truth" shirts. A poster said, "If the Bilderbergers are here . . . who's running hell?" Another said "Only Evil Is Done in Secret."

"Once again, members of the local mainstream news organizations, including *The Washington Post* and *The Washington Times*," said the protest participant, "did not have a single word printed on the most important news event in the area."

On the Internet webzine *Slate* on June 9, 2008, Jack Shafer wrote, "As in previous years, Bilderberg critics are berating the mainstream press for observing a 'blackout' of a group they believe directs a secret, shadow government."

Noting that protestors staked out the elite at the hotel's entrance and had placed "surveillance" videos inside and outside the minimum-security facility before the event commenced, Shafer continued, "About this much the Bilderberg critics are right: the mainstream media ignored Bilderberg 2008. According to [Internet sites] Nexis, Wonkette and Raw Story noted the event and the critics' objections on the Web. A simple Web search produces Bilderberg detractors Alex

Jones and Jim Tucker sounding their alarms. And about this, too, the Bilderberg critics are right: The meeting of 120 prominent world figures probably constitutes some kind of news. Yet to be fair to the mainstream press, it's tough to report from a private gathering locked down tight by professional security."

Recognizing that Bilderberg organizers "expect participants to keep the weekend's discussions off the record," Shafer observed that "private groups meet in almost every town in the world for confidential chats. It's the way of the world."

"What do you suppose would result," Shafer asked, "if *The Washington Post* had assigned a reporter to Chantilly's luminary jamboree? The Associated Press sent a reporter to cover the 1978 Bilderberger session in Princeton, N.J. but all he filed was a scene piece describing men in gray suits and sunglasses chasing him away from the off-limits grounds of the Henry Chauncey Conference Center."

In that dispatch AP's Steve Hindy wrote, "Kissinger casually strolled around a small man-made pond Saturday, coming within a few feet of the road leading into the complex He circled the pond twice, first with a gray-haired pipe-smoking man and then with a younger man. Kissinger appeared grave and attentive while the men talked of things like 'range limitations.' Kissinger looked annoyed and declined comment when approached by a reporter."

"And yet the 'mainstream press' could hardly be accused of blacking out Bilderberg," said Shafer. He cited *The New York Times* mentioning Bilderberg "a couple dozen times since 1981, and other pieces in *The Washington Post*, *Chicago Tribune*, and *The Boston Globe*.

"Of course, Bilderberg critics don't want to read mentions in the press," Shafer wrote.

"They want to see confirmation of their theories that the group operates in a sinister, behind-the-scenes fashion to exploit the powerless and throttle liberty."

How, exactly, are reporters supposed to do that, Shafer asked, when the critics rarely provide falsifiable evidence of Bilderberg malevolence? Would a shadow government, should it exist, really convene annually at a hotel to hash out the world's fate? Would it really issue a press release about its latest meeting? Would it routinely assume the security risks of inviting new blood in? Couldn't the notorious Bilderberger Conrad Black negotiate his way out of prison by exposing the group? Or is Bilderberg so powerful that it controls the federal prison system too? It largely limits its attendees to North Americans and Europeans. Are the Japanese, the Indians, Chinese, Brazilians, Australians, South Koreans, and Singaporeans so timid that they stand aside and let the Bilderbergers have their way with the world without making a peep?"

Letting the press in for a closer look at what goes on, Shafer suggested, "would go a long way to reduce the shouting while preserving the group's right to think out loud."

Because *Slate* is owned by the Washington Post Company, and its CEO, Donald Graham, has been a regular Bilderberg attendee, the conspiracy theorists dismissed the *Slate* article as nothing more than "a puff piece" providing favorable Bilderberg propaganda.

Despite any documented evidence that the Bilderberg Group had been plotting a New World Order since 1954, the belief persists that the purpose of the annual gatherings is to do just that. While Bilderberg watchers offer the EU as proof of progress toward a global government, history records that the movement toward Europe's unification grew out of the devastation wreaked by World War II, a need for solidarity in the face of a threat from the Soviet Union, and a desire to eliminate barriers to economic growth. Although conspiracy theorists attribute globalization to Bilderberg plotters, history shows that the phenomenon has been the result of dramatic advances in communication and technologies that have not only shrunk the world but required a merging of commerical and national interests. Those who view NAFTA as the first step toward elimination of U.S. sovereignty and creation of a

North American Union fail to recognize that the free-trade agreement has benefited the economies of the three countries.

Bilderberg watchers have also failed to recognize that the imposition of a global government, even in stages, by a group of men, however rich or powerful in their fields, in a world in which the majority of nations are democratic, is improbable. Despite great pressures to create an EU with a continental government, there was enormous opposition from the British, the French, and even the Irish, resulting in limitations on the power of the European parliament and commission in Brussels. That U.S. politicians would go along with the surrender of American sovereignty is highly implausible, as demonstrated in the 2008 election by Hillary Clinton and Barack Obama's vows to alter or even abandon NAFTA.

The desire to create a New World Order has been a goal of dreamers, despots, and demagogues throughout recorded history, from Alexander the Great and Pax Romana to the Holy Roman Empire, Hitler, the Soviet Union, and the United Nations. In every age, there has always been an attempt to remake the world through force or with ideas. Yet the annals of our history are littered with failures. The world chronicle is also strewn with instances in which organizations that were accused of being New World Order conspiracies proved to be harmless. In nineteenth-century America it was the Freemasons. They were so feared that a political party (the Anti-Masons) was formed in an attempt to keep Freemasons from gaining control of the government, and a national anti-Mason movement almost succeeded in driving Freemasonry out of existence. While there was no evidence that the Freemasons were (or are) a conspiracy to establish a Masonic World Order, many people who believe it find all kinds of "proof," from U.S. presidents and government officials who were (or are) Masons to so-called Masonic symbolism all over Washington, DC, and on the dollar bill.

While Daniel Estulin and Jim Tucker have published books on the Bilderberg Group, the majority of those who sound alarms about its activities do so via the Internet. In a few instances, they venture beyond the realm of internationalists, such as Rockefeller, Kissinger, Brzezinksi, CEOs of global corporations, political idealists, and power seekers. Some of the people who suspect the Bilderberg Group of being a conspiracy to rule the world also contend that the Group knows of the existence of space aliens.

One believer contended that after the world was "electrified by newspaper headlines and photos of squadrons of UFOs flying repeatedly over Washington," President Eisenhower ordered the CIA's Office of Scientific Intelligence (OSI) to determine if UFOs were really interstellar vehicles. "A year later, in April, 1954, said this writer, Eisenhower made a secret trip to Muroc Field (now Edwards Air Force Base), in the California desert, accompanied by generals, reporter Franklin Allen of the Hearst Newspapers Group, Los Angeles Catholic bishop James McIntyre, and others." Ostensibly on a golfing vacation, Ike "was spirited over to Muroc one night," while reporters were fed the cover story that he had a toothache and needed to see a dentist. "While at Muroc Air Field, Eisenhower was present while one of the extraterrestrial discs landed. Several "Star Visitors" emerged to converse with him and the generals. The extraterrestrials requested that Eisenhower make the public aware of the extraterrestrial contact with Earth forthwith. The president protested that humans were not ready and needed time to be prepared for adjusting to this stupendous reality.

By the end of the following month, May 1954, this story goes, Eisenhower's CIA director Walter Bedell Smith, Prince Bernhard, David Rockefeller, and other top world financiers, later secretary of state Dean Rusk, later british minister of defense Denis Healey, and other Western power leaders, convened the inaugural meeting of the Bilderberg Group. One of the early items on the Bilderberg agenda was said to be "extraterrestrial contact."

Some Bilderberg watchers believe that the Group knows of the existence of corpses of alien beings and their spacecraft that are stored by the Air Force, as well as the origins of the so-called crop circles that have mysteriously appeared in corn and wheat fields.

Among the websites and bloggers on the subject of a Bilderberg conspiracy there occasionally appears a doubter. One wrote, "Here is the thing that always cracks me up about conspiracy theories: You can't get that many people to agree on what to have for lunch, let alone two-to-three days once per year, come up with some sort of concerted policy on the important issues. It is merely a discussion forum. No more, no less."

Another asserted, "No secret decisions are made, no vast conspiracies launched, just a bunch of people sitting around and sharing information." A very dubious observer bluntly declared, "If you wish to prove some vast conspiracy, you have a high bar to clear when it comes to proving this. You would have to have a witness, or participant actively admitting this kind of wheeling and dealing is going on. Put up or shut up. I want proof."

Instead of proof of a Bilderberg conspiracy to rule the world, what has been presented is speculation and theorizing.

Other conspiracy doubters on the Internet said: "Any meeting of important people is by definition important, since important people don't got to unimportant meetings."

"What these people do is give each other insider/Master-of-the-Universe tips on directions and tendencies, where to invest/not-invest, since they are all wealthy capitalists primarily interested in getting wealthier."

"Does any fool think that these people have anybody's interest in mind, other than their own?"

These comments on the Bilderberg Group were offered prior to the financial crisis that was described to the leaders of Congress on September 18, 2008, by Secretary of the Treasury Paulson and Federal Reserve chairman Bernanke. Because both men had recently attended a Bilderberg meeting, suspicions arose among Bilderberg critics that the banking crisis had been created to forward the Bilderberg goal of economic globalization and a New World Order in which power would be concentrated in the hands of a few bankers.

When Paulson presented Congress with a plan in which he as treasury secretary would be authorized to expend $700 billion to "bail out" banks and Wall Street firms by acquiring their "bad debts" in the form of defaulted mortgages, conservative Republicans and some Democrats in the House of Representatives described the bill as socialism and voted not to approve it, causing the initial bill to fail. Opponents of the Paulson-Bernanke plan to rescue the banks and Wall Street firms argued that in free-market capitalism, the troubled entities should be allowed to fail. Bilderberg critics saw the Paulson-Bernanke plan as one more step on the road to financial globalization in which national sovereignty would vanish.

As evidence that the Bilderberg Group was succeeding, its opponents pointed to the credit crisis of 2008, the EU, NAFTA, the expansion of NATO, international corporations, the collapse of immigration enforcement in the United States, and internationalization of banking.

Are these the inevitable results of advances in technology, or are they part of a plan devised by scheming, powerful men (and an occasional woman) who meet in secret and call themselves the Bilderberg Group?

You decide.

Bilderberg Meeting Dates and Places

1954 (May 29–31) Hotel de Bilderberg in Oosterbeek, Netherlands

1955 (March 18–20) Hotellerie Du Bas-Breau, Barbizon, France

1955 (September 23–25) Grand Hotel Sonnenbichl, Garmisch-Partenkirchen, West Germany

1956 (May 11–13) Hotel Store Kro, Fredensborg, Denmark

1957 (February 15–17) King and Prince Hotel, St. Simons Island, Georgia

1957 (October 4–6) Grand Hotel Palazzo della Fonte, Fiuggi, Italy

1958 (September 13–15) The Palace Hotel, Buxton, England

1959 (September 18–20) Cinar Hotel, Yessilköy, Istanbul, Turkey

1960 (May 28–29) Palace Hotel in Burgenstock, Nidwalden, Switzerland

1961 (April 21–23) Manoir St. Castin in Lac-Beauport, Quebec, Quebec, Canada

1962 (May 18–20) Grand Hotel Saltsjobaden, Saltsjobaden, Sweden

1963 (May 29–31) Cannes, France

1964 (March 20–22) Williamsburg, Virginia

1965 (April 2–4) Villa d'Este in Cernobbio, Italy

1966 (March 25–27) Nassauer Hof Hotel Wiesbaden, Wiesbaden, West Germany

1967 (March 31–April 2) Cambridge, England

1968 (April 26–28) Mont Tremblant, Quebec, Canada

1969 (May 9–11) Hotel Marienlyst in Helsingør, Denmark

1970 (April 17–19) Grand Hotel Quellenhof, Bad Ragaz, Switzerland

1971 (April 23–25) Woodstock Inn, Woodstock, Vermont

1972 (April 21–23) Reserve di Knokke-Heist, Knokke, Belgium

1973 (May 11–13) Grand Hotel Saltsjobaden, Saltsjobaden, Sweden

1974 (April 19–21) Hotel Mont d'Arbois, Megeve, France

1975 (April 22–24) Golden Dolphin Hotel in Cessme, Izmir, Turkey

1976 no conference. The 1976 Bilderberg conference was planned for
April at The Homestead in Hot Springs, Virginia. Because of the
Lockheed scandal involving Prince Bernhard, it was cancelled.

1977 (April 22–24) Paramount Imperial Hotel, Torquay, England

1978 (April 21–23) Chauncey Conference Center, Princeton, New
Jersey

1979 (April 27–29) Grand Hotel Sauerhof in Baden bei Wien, Austria

1980 (April 18–20) Dorint Sofitel Quellenhof Aachen, Aachen, West
Germany

1981 (May 15–17) Palace Hotel in Burgenstock, Nidwalden, Switzerland

1982 (May 14–16) Rica Park Hotel Sandefjord, Sandefjord, Norway

1983 (May 13–15) Fairmont Le Chateau Montebello, Montebello,
Quebec, Canada

1984 (May 11–13) Grand Hotel Saltsjobaden, Saltsjobaden, Sweden

1985 (May 10–12) Doral Arrowwood Hotel, Rye Brook, New York

1986 (April 25–27) Gleneagles Hotel, Gleneagles, Auchterarder, Scotland

1987 (April 24–26) Villa d'Este, Cernobbio, Italy

1988 (June 3–5) Interalpen-Hotel Tyrol, Telfs-Buchen, Austria

1989 (May 12–14) Gran Hotel de La Toja, Isla de La Toja, Spain

1990 (May 11–13) Harrison Conference Center, Glen Cove, New York

1991 (June 6–9) Steigenberger Badischer Hof Hotel, Schlosshotel
Bühlerhöhe, Bühl (Baden) in Baden-Baden, Germany

1992 (May 21–24) Royal Club Évian Hotel, Ermitage Hotel, Évian-les-Bains, France

1993 (April 22–25) Nafsika Astir Palace Hotel, Vouliagmeni, Greece

1994 (June 2–5) Kalastajatorppa Hotel, Helsinki, Finland

1995 (June 8–11) Palace Hotel, Burgenstock, Nidwalden, Switzerland

1996 (May 30–June 2) CIBC Leadership Centre, King City, Canada

1997 (June 12–15) Pine Isle Resort, Lake Lanier, Georgia

1998 (May 14–17) Turnberry Hotel, Turnberry, Scotland

1999 (June 3–6) Caesar Park Hotel Penha Longa, Sintra, Portugal

2000 (June 1–4) Chateau Du Lac Hotel, Genval, Brussels, Belgium

2001 (May 24–27) Hotel Stenungsbaden, Stenungsund, Sweden

2002 (May 30–June 2) Westfields Marriott, Chantilly, Virginia

2003 (May 15–18) Trianon Palace Hotel, Versailles, France

2004 (June 3–6) Grand Hotel des Iles Borromees, Stresa, Italy

2005 (May 5–8) Dorint Sofitel Seehotel Überfahrt, Rottach-Egern, Germany

2006 (June 8–11) Brookstreet Hotel in Kanata, Ottawa, Ontario, Canada

2007 (May 31–June 3) Ritz-Carlton Hotel, Istanbul, Turkey.

2008 (June 7–9) Westfields Marriott, Chantilly, Virginia

American Bilderbergers

The following is a partial listing of persons who are known or reported to have attended at least one Bilderberg Group meeting:

Name	Present and/or Past Title/ Affiliation
Acheson, Dean	Secretary of State
Aaron, David I.	Deputy National Security Advisor
Allison, Graham	Kennedy School of Government, Harvard
Anderson, John B.	Congressman, presidential candidate
Andreas, Dwayne	Chairman, Archer Daniels Midland Co.
Baker, James	Secretary of State
Ball, George W.	State Department
Barone, Michael	Editor, *Almanac of American Politics*
Bartley, Robert Leroy	Editor, *The Wall Street Journal*
Bayh, Evan	Senator
Bell, David Elliot	Executive vice president, Ford Foundation
Bentsen, Lloyd	Senator, vice-presidential candidate
Berger, Sandy	National Security Advisor

Bernanke, Ben S.	Chairman, Federal Reserve Board
Binkley, Nicholas B.	Bankamerica Corp., San Diego
Black, Conrad	Financier
Black, Shirley Temple	Ambassador
Blackwill, Robert	National Security Council
Blankfein, Lloyd C.	Chairman, Goldman Sachs & Co.
Boyd, Charles G.	Business Executives for National Security
Brademas, John	Congressman
Bradley, Bill	Senator
Bradley, Tom	Mayor, Los Angeles
Brady, Nicholas	Secretary of Treasury
Bremmer, Ian	President, Eurasia Group (USA)
Brooke, Edward	Senator
Bryan, John H.	Chairman, Sara Lee Corp.
Brzezinski, Zbigniew	National Security Advisor
Buckley, William F., Jr.	Magazine editor, columnist
Bundy, McGeorge	National Security Advisor
Camps, Miriam	State Department
Case, Clifford	Senator
Chaffee, John	Senator
Church, Frank	Senator
Cisler, Walker Lee	Defense Department European Command
Clinton, Bill	President, governor of Arkansas
Clinton, Hillary	Presidential candidate, senator
Collins, Timothy C.	CEO, Rippling Holdings, LLC (USA)
Cook, Donald (Don)	*Los Angeles Times*
Cooper, Richard Newell	Harvard University
Corzine, Jon	Senator, governor of New Jersey

NAME	PRESENT AND/OR PAST TITLE/ AFFILIATION
Dam, Kenneth	Deputy Secretary of Treasury
Davis, Lynn E.	State Department
Deutch, John M.	Director, CIA
Dewey, Thomas E.	Governor of New York, presidential candidate
Dillon, C. Douglas	Secretary of Treasury
Dodd, Christopher	Senator
Donilon, Thomas E.	State Department
Dullara, Charles H.	State Department
Dyson, Esther	Chairman, Edventure Holdings, Inc.
Edwards, John	Senator, vice-presidential candidate
Eizenstat, Stuart	Deputy Secretary of Treasury
Espy, Mike	Secretary of Agriculture
Evans, Daniel J.	Senator
Feinstein, Dianne	Senator
Florio, James	Governor of New Jersey
Foley, Thomas	Speaker of the House
Ford, Gerald R.	President
Ford, Henry II	President, Ford Motor Company
Fraser, Donald M.	Congressman
Freeman, Charles W., Jr.	Defense Department
Friedman, Stephen James	Goldman Sachs & Co.
Friedman, Thomas	*The New York Times*
Frelinghuysen, Peter	Congressman
Fulbright, William	Senator
Gallagher, Cornelius Edward	Congressman
Geithner, Timothy F.	Federal Reserve Bank of New York

Gergen, David	Presidential advisor, commentator
Gerstner, Louis, Jr.	Chairman, IBM
Gigot, Paul	Editorial page editor, *The Wall Street Journal*
Glickman, Dan	Congressman
Goodpaster, Andrew	Defense Department, presidential advisor
Graham, Donald E.	Chairman and CEO, Washington Post Company
Greenberg, Maurice R.	Banker
Gregg, Donald	Ambassador
Grossman, Marc	The Cohen Group, Under Secretary of State
Grunwald, Henry Anatole	Editor-in-chief, *Time* magazine
Haas, Richard N.	President, Council on Foreign Relations
Hagel,Chuck	Senator
Haig, Alexander	General, Secretary of State
Hamilton, Lee	Congressman
Harris, Fred R.	Senator
Hart, Peter	Peter D. Hart Research Associates
Hauge, Gabriel	Presidential advisor
Heburgh, Theodore	President, University of Notre Dame
Heinz, H. John III	H. J. Heinz Company, senator
Herter, Christian	Secretary of State
Holbrooke, Richard	Ambassador to United Nations
Hubbard, Allan B.	Assistant to the president for economic policy
Hunter, Robert E.	Congressman
Jackson, Henry	Senator
Jacobs, Kenneth	Lazard Frères & Co.
Javits, Jacob K.	Senator
Jeter, Howard F.	Ambassador to Liberia

NAME	PRESENT AND/OR PAST TITLE/ AFFILIATION
Johnson, James A.	Vice chairman, Perseus, LLC (USA)
Johnson, Joseph E.	President, Carnegie Endowment for Peace
Johnston, Bennett	Senator
Jones, James Robert	Congressman
Jordan, Vernon	Senior managing director, Lazard Frères & Co.
Kann, Peter Robert	Chairman, Dow Jones, *The Wall Street Journal*
Kassebaum, Nancy	Senator
Kean, Thomas	Governor of New Jersey
Kennedy, David M.	Secretary of the Treasury
Kimmitt, Robert M.	Deputy Secretary of Treasury
Kimsey, James V.	America Online
Kissinger, Henry	Secretary of State, Kissinger Associates.
Knoppers, Antoine T.	Senior vice president, Merck & Co.
Krauthammer, Charles	Columnist
Kravis, Henry	Kohlberg Kravis Roberts & Co.
Kravis, Marie-Josee	Hudson Institute
Kristol, William (Bill)	Editor/publisher, *The Weekly Standard*
Krogh, Peter F.	Dean, Georgetown School of Foreign Service
LaFalce, John	Congressman
Lapham, Lewis	*Harper's Magazine*
Levy, Walter James	Johns Hopkins University
Lord, Winston	Cmbassador to China
Luti, William J.	National Security Council
McAuliffe, Terry	Chairman, Democratic National Committee

McCloy, John J. II	Commander, U.S. Air Force European Command
McCracken, Paul Winston	University of Michigan
McDonough, William J.	President, Federal Reserve Bank of New York
McHenry, Donald	UN Ambassador
McNamara, Robert	Secretary of Defense, president, World Bank
Mathews, Jessica T.	Carnegie Endowment for Peace
Mathias, Charles	Senator
Mehlman, Ken	Chairman, Republican National Committee
Meyer, Cord	Central Intelligence Agency
Mitchell, George	Senator
Mondale, Walter	Vice President, U.S. Senator
Morse, F. Bradford	UN undersecretary
Nitze, Paul	Presidential advisor
Nunn, Sam	Senator
Nye, Benjamin H.	Executive secretary, Treasury Department
Pataki, George	Governor of New York
Paulson, Henry	Chairman, Goldman Sachs & Co., Secretary of the Treasury
Pell, Claiborne	Senator
Perle, Richard	Assistant Secretary of State
Perlstein, Norman	Time Warner
Perry, Rick	Governor of Texas
Perry, William J.	Secretary of Defense
Petersen, Charles A.	National Security Council
Pickering, Thomas R.	Ambassador to UN, USSR
Powell, Colin	Secretary of State
Pressler, Larry	Senator

NAME	PRESENT AND/OR PAST TITLE/AFFILIATION
Quayle, Dan	Vice President
Rattner, Steve	Lazard Frères & Co.
Reed, Ralph	Christian Coalition
Richardson, Bill	Governor of New Mexico, Secretary of the Interior
Rice, Condoleeza	Secretary of State
Riegle, Donald W.	Senator
Rockefeller, David	Bilderberg founding member, Chase Bank
Rockefeller, Jay	Senator
Rockefeller, Nelson	Vice President, Governor of New York
Rockefeller, Sharon Percy	WETA-TV (PBS), Washington, DC
Ross, Dennis	Ambassador, Middle East negotiator
Rostow, Walt	National Security Advisor
Rubin, Robert E.	Secretary of the Treasury
Rumsfeld, Donald	Secretary of Defense
Rusk, Dean	Secretary of State
Samuelson, Paul Anthony	New York University
Schmidt, Eric	CEO, Google
Scott, Hugh	Senator
Scowcroft, Brent	National Security Advisor
Scully, Robert W.	Morgan Stanley
Sheinkman, Jack	Amalgamated Clothing and Textile Workers
Silverberg, Kristen	Bureau of International Organization Affairs, State Department
Soderberg, Nancy	Deputy assistant to the president
Soros, George	President, Soros Fund Management

Sparkman, John	Senator
Stahl, Lesley	CBS/*60 Minutes*
Steinberg, James	National Security aAdvisor
Stephanopoulos, George	Senior advisor to President Bill Clinton
Stevenson, Adlai E.	Governor of Illinois, presidential candidate
Strauss, Robert S.	Chairman, Democratic National Committee
Sulzberger, Cyrus Leo	*The New York Times*
Summers, Lawrence	Secretary of the Treasury
Sununu, John	Governor of New Hampshire
Taurel, Sidney	Chairman and CEO, Eli Lilly and Company
Thiel, Peter A.	President, Clarium Capital Management
Thiessen, Marc	Aide to Senator Jesse Helms
Tower, John	Senator
Trotman, Alexander J.	Chairman, Ford Motor Company
Tuthill, John Willis	Ambassador to Brazil
Tyson, Laura D'Andrea	Council of Economic Advisors
van Vorst, I. Bruce	Senior correspondent, *Time* magazine
Vance, Cyrus	Secretary of State
Vinocur, John	*International Herald Tribune*
Vogel, Ezra F.	Harvard University
Volcker, Paul	Chairman, Federal Reserve Board
Weber, Vin	Congressman
Whitman, Christie Todd	Governor of New Jersey, Environmental Protection Agency
Wicker, Thomas	*The New York Times*
Wilder, L. Douglas	Governor of Virginia

NAME	PRESENT AND/OR PAST TITLE/ AFFILIATION
Will, George	Columnist
Williams, Lynn Russell	International president, United Steel Workers
Wilson, Ross	Ambassador to Turkey
Wisner, Frank G. II	Ambassador to Egypt
Wohlstetter, Albert J.	*The Wall Street Journal*
Wolfensohn, James D.	Chairman, Wolfensohn and Company
Wolfowitz, Paul	President, World Bank, presidential advisor
Wriston, Walter Bigelow	Chairman, Citicorp
Zelikow, Philip D.	Counselor, State Department, 9/11 Commission
Zoellick, Robert	President, World Bank, Deputy Secretary of State
Zuckerman, Mortimer B.	Publisher, *New York Daily News, U.S. News & World Report*

BILDERBERG PRESS RELEASE

Except for the number of the meeting date, place, and subjects of discussion listed in the first paragraph, this is the standard press release issued each year prior to the meeting.

The 46th Bilderberg Meeting will be held in Turnberry, Scotland, May 14–17, 1998, to discuss the Atlantic Relationship in a Time of Change. Among others the Conference will discuss NATO, Asian Crisis, EMU, Growing Military Disparity, Japan, Multilateral Organizations, Europe's social model, Turkey, EU/US Market Place.

Approximately 120 participants from North America and Europe will attend the discussions. The meeting is private in order to encourage frank and open discussion. Bilderberg takes its name from the hotel in the Netherlands where the first meeting took place in May 1954. That meeting grew out of the concern on both sides of the Atlantic that the industrialized democracies in Europe and North America were not working together as closely as they should on matters of critical importance. It was felt that regular, off-the-record discussions would contribute to a better understanding of the complex forces and major trends affecting Western nations.

What is unique about Bilderberg as a forum is the broad cross-section of leading citizens, in and out of government, that are assembled for nearly three days of purely informal discussion about topics of current concern especially in the fields of foreign affairs and the international economy, the strong feeling among participants that in view of the differing attitudes and experiences of their nations, there is a continuous, clear need to develop an understanding in which these concerns can be accommodated, and the privacy of the meetings, which have no purpose other than to allow participants to speak their minds openly and freely.

To ensure full discussion, individuals representing a wide range of political and economic points of view are invited. Two thirds of the participants come from Europe and the remainder from the United States and Canada. Within this framework, on average about one third are from the government sector and the remaining two thirds from a variety of fields including finance, industry, labor, education and the media. Participants are solely invited for their knowledge, experience and standing and with reference to the topics on the agenda.

All participants attend Bilderberg in a private, and not in an official, capacity.

Participants have agreed not to give interviews to the press during the meeting. In contacts with the news media after the conference, it is an established rule that no attribution should be made to individual participants of what was discussed during the meeting.

There will be no press conference. A list of participants is appended.

Further Reading

Aldrich, Nelson W. *Old Money: The Mythology of America's Ruling Class.* New York: Knopf, 1988.

Allen, Gary. *The Rockefeller File.* Seal Beach, CA: '76 Press, 1976.

————. *Say "No!" to the New World Order.* Seal Beach, CA: Concord Press, 1987.

Bird, Kai. *The Chairman: John J. McCloy, The Making of the American Establishment.* New York: Simon & Schuster, 1992.

Brinkley, Douglas, and Clifford Hackett, eds. *Jean Monnet: The Path to European Unity.* New York: Palgrave MacMillan, 1992.

Burch, Philip. H. *Elites in American History.* 3 vols. New York: Holmes & Meier, 1980.

Callahan, David. *Dangerous Capabilities: Paul Nitze and the Cold War.* New York: HarperCollins 1990.

Collier, Peter, and David Horowitz. *The Rockefellers: An American Dynasty.* New York: Holt, Rinehart & Winston, 1976.

Domhoff, G. William. *Who Rules America Now?: A View for the '80s.* Englewood Cliffs, NJ: Prentice-Hall, 1983.

Duchene, François. *Jean Monnet: The First Statesman of Interdependence.* New York: Norton, 1994.

Estulin, Daniel. *The True Story of the Bilderberg Group.* Waterville, OR: Trine-Day, 2007.

Fosdick, Raymond B. *John D. Rockefeller, Jr.: A Portrait.* New York: Harper & Brothers, 1956.

Harr, John Ensor, and Peter J. Johnson. *The Rockefeller Century.* New York: Scribner's, 1988.

Heald, Tim. *Old Boy Networks: Who We Know and How We Use Them.* New York: Ticknor & Fields, 1984.

Johnson, George. *Architects of Fear: Conspiracy Theories and Paranoia in American Politics.* Los Angeles: Tarcher, 1983.

Lundberg, Ferdinand. *The Rich and the Super-Rich: A Study in the Power of Money Today.* New York: Lyle Stuart, 1968.

————. *The Rockefeller Syndrome.* Secaucus, NJ: Lyle Stuart, 1975.

Mills, C. Wright. *The Power Elite.* New York: Oxford University Press, 1956.

Pastor, Robert A. *Toward a North American Community.* Washington, DC: Institute for International Economics, 2001.

Perloff, James. *The Shadows of Power: The Council on Foreign Relations and the American Decline.* Appleton, WI: Western Islands, 1988.

Pijl, Kees. van der. *The Making of an Atlantic Ruling Class.* London: Verso Press, 1984.

Quigley, Carroll. *The Anglo-American Establishment.* New York: Books in Focus, 1981.

Rockefeller, David. *Memoirs.* New York: Random House, 2002.

Ross, Robert Gaylon, Sr. *Who's Who of the Elite: Members of the Bilderbergs, Council on Foreign Relations & Trilateral Commission.* Spicewood, TX: RIE, 2002.

Sklar, Holly, ed. *Trilateralism: The Trilateral Commission and Elite Planning for World Management.* Boston: South End Press, 1980.

Sutton, Antony, and Patrick Wood. *Trilaterals over Washington.* 2 vols. Scottsdale, AZ: August Corp., 1978–81.

Tucker, James P., Jr. *Jim Tucker's Bilderberg Diary.* Washington, DC: American Free Press, 2005.

INDEX